Always Loved

GRIEVING THE LOSS OF A BABY

Original Edition

Find Your Way Publishing, Inc.
PO BOX 667
Norway, Maine

Always Loved

Grieving the Loss of a Baby

Copyright © 2015 Melissa Eshleman

First Edition

Published by Find Your Way Publishing, Inc.
PO BOX 667
Norway, ME 04268 U.S.A.
www.findyourwaypublishing.com

All rights reserved. No part of this book may be reproduced, stored in a retrieval system or transmitted in any form or by any means, electronic, mechanical, photocopying, recording, or otherwise, without the written permission of the publisher.

The stories contained in this book have been edited, yet not so to distort or lose any intended emotion or meaning submitted by its contributor, used by permission.

Scripture quotations are taken from the King James Version of the Bible. Public domain.

Find Your Way Publishing, Inc.

First Edition, 2015
ISBN-13: 978-0-9849322-4-5
ISBN-10: 0-9849322-4-0
Library of Congress Control Number: 2015933395

Printed in the United States of America.

Dedication

To my children, here and there
To all who have loved and lost
To all who strive to make the world a better place

This book is dedicated to all who are making the best of every day; to those who face their struggles with wonder in their heart although it may be breaking; to those who share their stories and reach out a helping hand to others. We are all in this together, let us not forget that. And to those who trust in the power of love, and give it freely. We loved our children before they were even born. We couldn't help but love them. It was born from within. We will continue to love them for eternity, and we can be sure that they love us too. Love. What a powerful gift.

With Gratitude

Deepest thanks to the parents who had the courage to share their heartfelt experiences and stories. I am touched and honored to have worked with you. By your example and with your words, you have shown the rest of us that we are not alone. And that with faith, perseverance and hope, healing - although a work in progress - is a realistic goal to attain. It is my hope that you found some solace and healing as you bravely wrote about your loss. I believe our angels are with us, guiding us to be true to ourselves and helping us see the beauty in all things, including loss. I am truly grateful and wish you all the best.

Deep, humble appreciation goes to the Divine Source; my Great Creator, in whom I want to grow closer to every day. There are no words to describe the joy, wonder and awe I continue to feel as I study the Word of God. Thank you for always hearing my prayers, for easing my pain and heartaches, for washing away my worries, for teaching me to trust the Universe always, for sincere and endless forgiveness, and for endless blessings. I am moved and blessed by the daily miracles in my life.

Foreword

The obituary stated four days. I never really understood that. May 17, 2001 – May 20, 2001. Isn't that three days? It was counted as four individual days; the 17th, 18th, 19th, and 20th. I was happy for the fourth day, but his life was significant regardless. He was loved by so many people. Does that sound strange? That Lucas was loved by so many people even though he only lived for four days? It's amazing isn't it? There is no explanation for love; it just is. Lucas touched so many lives in the short time he was here on this earth. A short stay, yet a huge impact; he made an enormous difference.

Lucas died in our arms a few days after he was born. It was not suppose to happen that way. The emotions that raged through me during that time were overwhelming; an all-encompassing void that I didn't know what to do with. I've never felt so alone. I felt as though no one could possibly understand how empty I felt. Everyone seemed to be going about their business and I was lost in grief. I had no idea what to do or who to turn to. I finally found an online infant-loss group. I signed up to receive emails and for a year I just read posts from other grieving parents. Until one day, with a little apprehension, I finally shared my story. The group helped me with my grief; listening and responding to my emails, sharing their stories and reaching out with encouraging words of compassion and understanding. The group helped me realize that, at a time when I felt more alone than ever, I wasn't alone in my pain and heartache. A sense of comfort came over me that I hadn't experienced before. I realized that my experience and words were helping others. It was during that time that I realized I wanted to do something to help others who have, or will have to endure the grief and confusion that comes with losing an infant. So I decided to put a book together; a book that would include stories from people who have experienced the loss of a child, because for me that is what seemed to help the most. This is a clear and easy-to-understand book to help people and their families realize that they are not alone in their grief; a book of hope.

Losing Lucas has taken me on a journey that I wasn't expecting. I miss him, and what would have been, every day. Since his death, I can't help but look at things differently. Things that matter the most have become clearer; a bit of the fog has lifted. I have come to realize that the little things in life bring me the most joy....watching my children sleep, hearing my children laugh, my slippers, my first cup of coffee in the morning, a warm breeze on my face, the sound of the rain, being in nature, a hot bath...these simple things satisfy my soul. I'm appreciative of the simplest moments. I am continually learning to trust God and to have faith in all of it.

It is my hope that this book and the heartfelt stories shared by parents who have been there, will bring comfort to those who have suffered the loss of a pregnancy, an infant, a sibling, a grandchild; a loved one.

These pages offer sincere advice, encouragement and inspiration. May this book be a gentle reminder that although you may feel it, you are not alone; may you be blessed with peace and comfort.

*"Imagine a love so strong
that saying hello and goodbye
in the same day
was worth the sorrow."*

~ Unknown

Contents

About This Book i

1   Alexander Williamson 1
2   Crystal Yesenia Stephens 9
3   Will & Leo Rivera 15
4   Three Angels 25
5   Cooper Boudreau Carson & Carter Boudreau
    Scout Boudreau 35
6   Alfonso "Alfy" Anthony Vaccaro 47
7   Samuel Brian Mackey 61
8   Two Angels 79
9   Lucia Anne Massenzio 85
10 Eden Rose Gidwitz Santi 95
11 Collin Joseph MacGregor 101
12 Gabriella Rose Shen 107
13 Ceiliedh Madison Burger 113

14 Kaia and Ezra 123
15 Benjamin Spencer Klimaszewski 129
16 Lucas Edward Eshleman 137

Afterword 157
About Melissa Eshleman 159
Resources 161
Disclaimer 175

About This Book

This is not just a book of hope. It is a book about an incredible love that cannot be broken or severed. It is an easy-to-understand book that doesn't tell you how you should feel; rather it explains the many different experiences and feelings that can follow a miscarriage or infant loss. If you want to read all the way through from cover to cover you can, but it's also broken down in a way that can be used as a helpful and comforting reference or guide. Through other's stories, it offers guidance on how to deal with your emotions, how to keep your infants memory alive, along with other helpful and inspiring thoughts and ideas.

Coping with miscarriage or infant loss can be one of the most difficult trials in a person's life and one most of us are unprepared to face. Pregnancy and infant loss are the most unexpected losses; they don't fit into the natural order of life.

With miscarriage or infant loss, hopes and dreams are shattered before they can even begin. We've been taught to never give up on our dreams; to dream big and keep dreaming, that all of our hopes and dreams can be obtained if we don't quit. But what do you do when your dream has ended before it had the chance to come into being or to begin? The dream is over and even though you've always been taught to never lose sight of your dreams, there appears to be absolutely no hope. How do you obtain a dream that has literally died? What can be done? What's the next step when faced with such a loss?

This book is like having a caring and compassionate support group in the palm of your hands. You will be moved by the deep, emotional honesty of these stories. This book offers practical advice and suggestions. Some stories will touch you more than others. Trust your feelings and take what comes to you on your own time. Wherever you are, on this challenging yet miraculous journey, you'll find that although it feels like it, you are not alone in your grief. And you will gain a little more strength with each passing day.

If you have suffered the devastating loss of a miscarriage or infant loss, or if you love someone who has experienced such a loss, you will want to read each of these heartfelt stories. This book is about the dark, stormy clouds slowly breaking. The sun is peaking through and it will shine again. Together let's move forward toward healing.

Always Loved

GRIEVING THE LOSS OF A BABY

A Child of Mine

I'll lend you for a little time a child of mine, He said.
For you to love - while he lives
And mourn for when he's dead.

It may be six or seven months
Or twenty-two or three,
But will you, till I call him back,
Take care of him for Me?

He'll bring his smiles to gladden you,
And should this stay be brief
You'll have his lovely memories
as solace for your grief.

I cannot promise he will stay,
Since all from earth return,
But there are lessons taught down there
I want this child to learn.

I've looked this world over
In search for teachers true,
And from the throngs that crowd
Life's lanes, I have selected you.

Now will you give him all your love,
Nor count the labor vain,
Nor hate Me when I come to call
To take him back again.

I fancied that I heard them say,
Dear Lord, Thy will be done,
For all the love Thy child shall bring,
The risk of grief we'll run.

We'll shelter him with tenderness,
We'll love him while we may,
And for the happiness we've known
Forever grateful stay.

But should the angels call for him
Much sooner than we've planned,
We'll brave the bitter grief that comes
And try to understand.

~ Unknown

CHAPTER I

Alexander Williamson

July 13, 2004

My Story:
In 2004 I lost my son Alex. I have since had another son, Kyle, but Alex and the experience of his short time with me has left an everlasting impact on me as a person and as a father. I wrote for the "Tears Together" Newsletter back in 2009 and again in 2014, in which my stories were published. Shortly after I wrote the 2009 article, I read it at the "Walk to Remember" event in October, and was astounded by the amazing response I got from both Fathers and Mothers.

I'd like to share the article I wrote in 2009:

I have been contemplating the writing of this for five years now, and truly feel that it's now time. For those of you reading this, you have obviously gone through the same tragic experience that I have, and I cannot begin to fully express my sympathy for your loss. I know that you are angry, and asking "Why me, Why my child?", and no one understands that more than I do. My son Alexander Douglas Williamson was born still on July 13th 2004, and from that day forward my life has never been the same. It is a loss that only a handful of us understand, and can relate to.

We are a select group of people that have the unbearable task of saying we have lost a child. To many it is something they think can fade away over time, and we know that just isn't the case. We all mourn our loss in varied ways. To honor my son I tattooed his initials and footprints on my forearm; while you might have your child's footprint or picture on your mantle. Either way our loss is a unique circumstance that none of us had any control of.

So what do you do now you ask? All I can simply suggest is to try to take something from this loss. Don't walk around bitter and angry at those you are close to or complete strangers. Honor your child by going through life treating those as you want to be treated, and try to not use your loss as a crutch for anything that may go wrong. Don't cast blame on yourself or your spouse for it was never either one of your faults, and if you can see that, you should be able to weather the storm.

If my story helps and resonates with at least one person than my sons loss to me serves some sort of "Higher purpose". It is a subject that many tend to overlook, and don't realize the everlasting pain that those of us who have gone through it, experience daily.

Alex's little brother, Kyle and I, every year on his birthday, go visit him at the cemetery, and make it a point to go out and partake in an activity that I think Alex would have liked to do with Kyle and I. I believe it's important to take what is an overwhelmingly emotional day every year and turn it into a positive.

I believe that these children were given to us parents for reasons we will never truly know, but THERE IS A REASON!!!!! I know my son helped to knock me back on a better path than what I was heading into, and gave me the courage to step out and try to pursue my dreams. I hope that if any of you need anything in the future you will contact me; I'd love to have the chance to help any of you in any way possible. I send my love to you all and look forward to getting the chance to talk to some of you soon. Take care and God Bless.

And here is the article I wrote in 2014:

Alex ~ 10 Years Later
A Dad's Perspective

It's almost hard to believe at times that it's been a decade since I last gazed upon my son Alex's face. Throughout the decade since he has passed it's been chock full of ups and downs, but one thing has remained a constant. I fight through only to realize that the best way to keep his memory alive and make any sense of his passing is to help others, like you. It doesn't matter if you are; A Mom, Dad, Aunt, Uncle, Grandma or Grandpa, ultimately the experience impacts all of us.

Alex's time on this planet was far too brief, yet his impact has been forever lasting. Initially after his passing, I was a VERY angry person. It seemed so many people were crawling out of the woodwork for information or to be there, yet not a single one of them understood or stuck around long enough to even attempt to put themselves in his Mother and My shoes. I began a long list of self destructive behaviors that I learned over time was nothing but a series of incredibly poor choices. This is my top five list of suggestions on how to make it through.

1. Never feel guilty for moving forward and appreciating what life has to offer. I don't believe our children or loved ones would disagree, that life has to move on.

2. Honor your child through helping others, or keeping their memories alive through friends and family. No matter how brief they were here, they mattered!

3. Find a spot to call your own that brings you peace and can emotionally clear your mind. It's important to have that one spot that calms your heart and soul.

4. Realize we are a small majority who have been through a tragic experience that many don't understand or fully grasp unless they have also

gone through it. The only way to change it is to educate them to the best of your ability.

5. Most importantly, as cliché' as it sounds, Go about treating others as you want to be treated. Nothing heals more than knowing you are being the best human being you can be, and it's a heck of a way to honor your child and loved ones you have lost.

In the ten years since Alex has passed, I have managed to always focus on how much more the good outweighs the bad in my life. In 2009 I had been lucky enough to be able to reach out to some of you through this newsletter, and went on to speak at the "Walk to Remember" event. I thank you for allowing me to do so, it has been a joy and truly humbling to me. Since that event, I was blessed to once again become a Father in October of 2010 to my amazing 3 & a 1/2 year old son Kyle. His Mom also has a 16 year old daughter Kailyn who I've had the joy of becoming a Father figure too.

Both of these kids have brought more joy into my life than I could have ever imagined. I've never held back from telling them both about Alex, and it brings me inner peace knowing they feel as connected to him as I do. We go out yearly now to celebrate Alex's Birthday, and it always consists of going to the cemetery, out to lunch, and then a fun activity of some sort. It is a great feeling to make the day about celebration, instead of mourning, and I believe that is what my son would have wanted.

It is also a must to surround yourselves with friends and family. I've been blessed to have a close knit family and group of friends spanning my entire life through just a few months ago, and they are always being supportive of me. To be able to bear such a private part of what makes me the man I am, is almost vital to retaining my sanity. Never be ashamed to talk about your child. If people shrug it off you will realize they simply aren't worth the time or effort. One of my best friends Lisa who was tragically taken last year said it best.... She would say to me "Life is what you make of it, Dougie, you can hold on to the anger and pain, or let it go and enjoy the ride"! Those words continually echo, because in her typical style, she made a concrete point. We all have one life and one shot to take in all of its experiences. Whether it's the beauty around us or the grief, it is all part of what makes this journey what it is. For me I learned awhile ago to let the anger go, and just simply do my best to keep Alex and his memory alive. Considering it is 10 years later, and here I am using his story to reach out and help as many of you as I possibly can, I'd have to say "Mission Accomplished"!!!

I hope Alex's story as well as my own have helped you and given you hope that there can and will be better days..... If you would like to contact me, feel free to do so.

Much love to you all.

~ Doug Williamson ~
dwilliamson_1978@ yahoo.com

***Blessed are those who mourn,
For they shall be comforted.***

Matthew 5:4

CHAPTER 2

Crystal Yesenia Stephens

January 14, 2010

My Story; in letter form to my baby:
I remember the day when the doctor told me you were a girl. It was in September of 2009. I was so excited I could not contain my happiness. I actually shouted it in the car as I was about to drive home. When I got there I dug out baby girl clothes I had been holding on to since my first pregnancy (with your older brother Cole).

It was in December, so as the month went on I started feeling lost. I kept counting your brothers. I would search all over the house like I misplaced something. Christmas came and went.

My next doctor's appt was January the 11th, which was also your Aunt Irma's Birthday. I knew and felt something was wrong, but I kept praying that it was not with you. Instead, just with what the day was. So, we (your brother Cole, a good friend and her daughter) got called in to see your progress. Doctor, put the fetal heart monitor on my belly. And we heard nothing. So, he tried to reassure me that everything was ok. He reached for the sonogram. He put it on my belly. What I saw on the screen was breath taking. I wanted to run screaming from the room. I just kept thinking it can't be. You were in the fetal position no movement, no heartbeat, and no activity. I was in shock. I was lost for words. Doctor looked at me and told me what was already obvious. I let him, but as he told me I ignored him. I looked at your brother and thought I NEED TO STAY STRONG! Lord, knows I wanted to act like a kid when someone took her favorite candy away.

They scheduled the induction on the 13th. I called and had it changed to the 14th. Until this day I do not know why. It just felt right. When I got to the hospital (a good friend again not the same one) she stayed with me for a while. Then, I was left alone to think about what was going on. They started inducing me. I could feel my body giving into the medication. After a while your Dad showed up. I forgot who was watching your brothers. I knew they were safe.

Around 10 pm you were born sleeping. I held you and talked to you. So, perfect so whole. I looked at you and counted your toes and fingers like I did for your older brothers. I saw you were whole. I could have sworn I saw your eyes flutter, but they did not open. I cried silent tears, for I know that no matter how hard it was no one would understand. I do not talk much about you, not because I don't love you, but because some people don't understand. I dislike the "it was meant to be", "she is in a better place" or "you will be with her one day" comments.

January the 14th is always so hard for me. As, I sit here crying my eyes and heart out. I just wish I could hold you. You do have a little brother that will also know of you. I love and miss you!

MOM! XOXOXO

PS You share your day with your Great, Great Grandmother on my side. ☺

~ Iraida Stephens (Salazar) ~

*How quietly he
tiptoed into our world.
Softly, only a moment
he stayed
but what an imprint
his footprints have left
upon our hearts.*

~ Unknown

CHAPTER 3

Will & Leo Rivera

August 27, 2013

Our story:
Two car seats, two cribs, two high chairs, two, two, two! When we found out we were having twins the dollar signs started adding up immediately. I was excited and equally nervous about the thought of having twins. Thankfully friends and family began offering baby gear and such. We began preparing for life with two infants.

Just when I started getting used to the idea of having twins, the nightmare began. I was having cramping which brought me to the hospital. The ultrasound technician took a long time scanning. She kept leaving the room and coming back after consulting with the doctor. My husband, Mark, and my mom were in the room with me and although they tried to reassure me that everything was ok, I knew in my heart it was not. The doctor finally came in the room and informed us that our sons had developed twin-to-twin transfusion syndrome or TTTS. They were identical twins sharing the same placenta and experiencing uneven blood flow. We would need to undergo a laser procedure to correct the blood flow. Doing nothing would not have a positive outcome for both boys so we quickly made plans. We were told about a few centers across the country that performed this unique procedure. A few days later Mark, myself, our 14 month old son Bennett, and my parents were on a flight from Chicago to Philadelphia. The doctors at this hospital had a high success rate so we were feeling hopeful. We went through several ultrasounds and saw that twin B was bigger with more fluid around him and twin A was smaller with not much room to move. Besides that they looked perfect with strong heartbeats.

A few days later I was scheduled for surgery. The procedure was successful and the doctors were able to correct the blood flow between the boys. However after I was coming out of the anesthesia, I felt a gush and knew something was not right. The doctors quickly realized my membranes had ruptured a small side effect that could occur due to the nature of the procedure. It was devastating to hear. My pregnant belly had gone down considerably and the ultrasound showed very little fluid around our babies. The doctor said it was rare but the fluid could build back up if the tear in my membrane were to heal on its own. In the meantime I was monitored for infection, I was on strict bed rest, and I continued to leak fluid. The final ultrasound with my beautiful boys showed their fateful outcome. The membrane had not sealed and twin A had a brain bleed. Shortly after, I felt a bigger gush and was told I was dilated. I was induced and endured the worst 15 hours of my life knowing I would be giving birth to my sons who would not live. Will was born at 8:50 am and Leo right after at 8:51am. They were both born alive and we were able to tell them we loved them. We sang to them, talked to them, and admired their precious faces. At 20 weeks old they were so tiny but everything about them was perfect. They were so beautiful! My parents as well as their big brother, Bennett, were able to meet them and hold them. To this day we treasure the precious time we did have with them.

The hardest part for me:
It was very difficult to labor for 15 hours knowing my sons were not going to live. I felt like I was being tortured. I couldn't rest and the clock was my enemy. I am a very religious person and this terrible event in my life has shaken my faith. We prayed so hard and had so many people praying for us, and I couldn't help feeling let down by God. We were so positive and hopeful through the entire experience and sometimes I still find it hard to be hopeful. I had begged God for a miracle, but we didn't get it. It's a harsh reality knowing we will never get to hug and kiss our sons and watch them grow up. Another difficult thing for me is seeing twins out in public. I think I'll always feel a little sad and jealous.

Helpful things from friends and family:
Receiving phone calls, flowers, or cards from friends let us know they were thinking about us. We appreciated people telling us that they were thinking about us and praying for us. It wasn't so helpful when people gave us cliché answers like "everything happens for a reason" or "it was God's plan." Because Will had a brain bleed, we were told by the doctor that he would be very sick and disabled if he were to survive. Some people told us that God took them to heaven so they wouldn't have to endure a difficult life. That comment saddened me. I felt that God had blessed us with twins and I was ready to care for them no matter what the circumstances. We were more than ready to love them unconditionally. Those responses weren't helpful when all we wanted was to have our sons with us.

My parents' were amazing through the whole process. They were there to help us deal with our emotions when we first found out the boys had TTTS. It was extremely helpful for Mark, Bennett, and I to have them with us for our almost 3 week stay in Philadelphia. My siblings were also a source of strength for us. Through our trials they always sent us uplifting text messages. My entire family helped us so much that I don't know where we would be without them.

Things that have helped me cope and deal with the heartache:
We met with an infant loss support group. My cousin and his wife also lost their son at 20 weeks and sharing

our stories with each other was comforting. We also met with a therapist to help us work through the grieving process. For me, I didn't like being alone so having a plan for each day and spending time with family and friends helped. My son, Bennett, was my saving grace. He kept me laughing and smiling. I knew I needed to function each day to take care of him. Without Bennett I would have been in a much darker place.

I have learned:

I have learned to cherish each day and find pleasure in the little things. I watch a beautiful sunset and think of my boys, I gaze at the stars and think of my boys, I enjoy a gentle snowfall and think of my boys. They are very much a part of my thought process each day. I have also learned that things are going to happen in my life that I can't control. We did everything we could to try to save our boys. I also try not to get upset over little issues anymore. In the grand scheme of life, most things are not a big deal.

How I keep the boys' memory alive:

Both Mark and I have tattoos in memory of our sons. It's of Will's left footprint and Leo's right with angel wings and halos. Mine is on my ankle and Mark's is on his arm. My brother and sister in law purchased 2 trees for us and had them planted in our backyard. They are Venus Dogwood trees and each spring they will bloom with white flowers. We are excited to watch the trees grow and bloom each year in remembrance of Will and

Leo. It was a very special gesture. We also have a wall in our house dedicated to the boys. We have a picture the staff at the hospital helped us make of Bennett's footprints in between Will and Leo's footprints along with Mark and my handprints. I have a necklace with angel wings and a halo and a family necklace with the birthstones of all my children. I like wearing jewelry that makes me think of my boys. We also add a sticker to our Christmas cards each year to represent Will and Leo. Whenever I sign birthday cards for people, I put a heart with their initials in the bottom corner. They will always be a part of our family.

Additional words:
To me, losing a child is one of the worst experiences a person can go through. Grieving the loss is very difficult and I felt it twice as much because I lost two children that day. We had lost my grandfather a few weeks before the nightmare began with the boys. I was very close with him and I was able to find some comfort knowing he was there to greet Will and Leo when they got to Heaven. He probably gave them one of his strong "Grandpa" hugs that we all miss so much. I know that he is loving them, teaching them to play baseball, and to snap their fingers. We decided to give them both the middle name Frank, after him. Although I desperately wish I could see my boys now, I have inner peace knowing I will see them again one day. I can wait…but I can't wait!

~ Christie Rivera ~

"Perhaps they are not stars, but rather openings in Heaven where the love of our lost ones pours through and shines down upon us to let us know they are happy." - Eskimo legend

They that sow in tears shall reap in joy.

Psalms 126:5

CHAPTER 4

Three Angels

First trimester losses in 2008, 2010, 2011

My story:
From the time I can remember, I wanted to be a mother. I remember changing my Cabbage Patch Kid's imaginary diaper, then slowly rocking her to sleep afterward. I remember stroller outings with my stuffed monkey, George. I even remember my Popple, who needed more mothering than you'd think, and that dreadful clown, whose balloons seemed to come alive in the deep hush of night.

For me, motherhood was never a question of if; it was only a question of when. I never worried about timing. I never considered that pregnancy might not be easy. That sometimes it might not happen. That other times it might end in heartbreak. I just thought I could wish a child into existence. That is was as easy and as beautifully complicated as that.

My husband and I waited longer than expected to start "trying" for a family. He had wanted to start on our wedding night, but suddenly I wasn't ready. I was scared of the responsibility, the sacred weight of motherhood, and secretly, I questioned if I'd be the mother I'd always dreamt of being. If I could live up to the kindness, patience and selfless love I'd shown my stuffed animals 20 years earlier.

In 2008, I became pregnant for the first time. It was a short-lived mix of emotion, a shooting star of questioning. But after the miscarriage was confirmed, I knew I had wanted that child. I knew that despite all my fears, I was ready.

Two years after our first loss, we were finally in a better place. A different place. A different country. Brazil. I knew I was expecting, but kept it quiet until my discomfort, dizziness and heightened emotions were too hard to hide. We made an appointment with a well-known and equally beloved ob/gyn and counted the days until our meeting.

Her first strike was arriving 40 minutes late, but I decided to look past it. Doctors, and good ones at that, were highly sought after in Criciuma. If people will wait, odds are she's that good, I thought.

After leading us back to her office and briefly discussing the reason for our visit, she led me to the stirrups. The exam was conducted in silence with the exception of the following: further, further down, wider and wider still. That was strike number two.

After removing her gloves she motioned for me to get dressed, and then stepped beyond the white curtain. Minutes later, reclining behind her desk, she told me I was not pregnant. I was, in fact, full of gas, for which she would write me a prescription. Oh, and the three-week late period…she'd write a prescription for that too.

Strike. Number. Three.

I was in disbelief. My husband could barely speak. I told her again I was sure I was expecting.

"I know pregnant women," she told me. "You are not one of them."

Now I hated her.

As she ushered us toward the reception desk I asked her plainly, "You're sure there's no chance I'm pregnant?"

"No chance," she responded, and walked away.

Through tears I told my husband two things. First: I was pregnant. Second: there was no way in hell I was taking any medication.

"You have to believe me," I said.

"You know I do," was his reply.

A week later we were in Florida. My sister was getting married and we were slowly making our way to Boston for the nuptials. I had bought two pregnancy tests the night before. The first was positive. And two days later the second was too. Afterward came the blood test. It was official: I was pregnant. I found myself with receiver in hand minutes after I heard the news. In my head, I was planning my verbal assault of the good doctor. She had it coming I told myself. But instead I put down the phone and hugged my husband.

Our euphoria was short-lived. One week after the wedding I started to bleed. Everything became hazy and pear-shaped. And I was scared of what I already knew.

At 12 weeks, our first ultrasound confirmed our baby had died three weeks earlier. The doctor called it a missed miscarriage and explained it as "embryo death without noticeable symptoms." I was still nauseous, still lightheaded, still glowing because my hormone levels hadn't started to fall. My body had tricked itself into believing I was still carrying a live embryo when in fact I was carrying a dead one.

I had to induce the abortion myself. Per Dr.'s orders, I was surrounded by bags of Doritos and Twizzlers as I waited for hours for the pressure, pressure, pressure and then the gush that would begin the process of passing my baby. My Dad held my left hand, my husband my right as the pains came, went, returned and intensified. I didn't look when I finally passed my baby. My husband made me promise. But I remember sitting there and feeling completely empty. Broken. Barren.

Arriving back home was painful. Friends and acquaintances approached with extended arms anxious to feel the life growing within me. And every time I pushed their hands away and shared our sorrow, it felt like the most vicious lie I'd ever told.

A few weeks passed and I had another checkup with another gynecologist. She also came highly recommended, but those words meant nothing to me then. Upon examination she told me that there was tissue that hadn't been passed. Tissue that could become infected.

THREE ANGELS

She strongly suggested a D&C. It was protocol in Brazil, but no longer in the States. I knew the risks, but feared the alterative, so we went ahead.

The morning of the procedure I was sent to wait in the maternity ward. Women with swollen bellies lined the back wall like birds on a telephone pole, each waiting for her scheduled C-section. Each waiting for her perfect little one to arrive. There was anxious chatter and laughter in the waiting room. Softly a lullaby began to play followed by a rush of souls to the far end of the room. That was the end with the large curtained window which, when opened, showcased the newest member of the human race, in Criciuma anyway.

I was suddenly hot and dizzy and sick to my stomach. I envied the way the women slid their hands up and down their bellies gently soothing the children within. And I envied the fathers passing out bubble gum cigars and shouting, "Meu filho. É meu filho," with tears and hints of fear in their eyes.

That should be us, I thought. Why isn't it us?

I did the only logical thing I could think of. I locked myself in the bathroom and bit my sleeve to muffle my cries.

When I was finally composed, I slid open the door. All eyes were on me.

"Are you the cureta?," an older woman asked.

I nodded.

"They're ready for you."

Our third loss happened 5 months later. I didn't enjoy a single minute of that pregnancy. Not even when we opened the results and unwrapped the hand stitched bib given in congratulations. I was already suffering. I was already waiting for something to go wrong. Because it would go wrong. I was sure of it.

Any twinge, any poke brought me back to the babies we lost, the pain we felt and the tears we shed. I made myself so anxious, so neurotic that when the miscarriage was confirmed, I wasn't surprised. I. was. relieved.

The hardest part for me:
The hardest part is thinking about trying again. And possibly losing again. I don't know if I could do it. I don't know if I could feel everything I felt—the betrayal, the humming womb that is suddenly quiet, the pain in parts of me I never knew I had—and somehow be okay. Again.

Helpful things from family and friends:
Their willingness to listen, their gentleness with my heart, and their prayers, which I know continue to reach Heaven.

Things that have helped me cope and deal with the heartache:
Writing has been a wonderful outlet for me. Sometimes it's just scribbling a fleeting thought or emotion on a napkin. Other times it's composing a post for a blog started last year. Whatever form it takes, writing keeps me connected to my truest self, which is someone who I've lost a few times. But I always find her. Always.

I have learned:
That I am much stronger than I thought and more blessed than I deserve.

How I keep my baby's memory alive:
We are nearly finished with my writing nook. It's a place I go mainly to write, but also to reflect and contemplate. On the right wall, is a hanging tribute to our children. While I don't have images of all three, I do have one of the second. When I write or sit or cry in this space, I feel them with me. Watching over me. As I know they are.

Additional words:
When we left Brazil, we packed up everything and either took it, shipped it or left it. We also packed up our emotions. I left my grief and guilt and longing in one of those boxes that stayed. And I boarded a plane and told myself that I was fine. That I was over it. That I should be over it. Because that's what people expect. And deep down that's what you hope and pray for. A sense of normalcy. A returning of self. A fullness blown into your empty places. But it doesn't come when you will it to. So you fear it never will.

During our last days there, my mother-in-law asked me if I still think about the losses. If they still haunt me like they once did.

I took a long time to respond. Not because I didn't know the answer but because I'd never been asked such a question. Because I think most people take my silence as an excuse for their own. And so no one speaks of it.

This is what I told her:

"I think of them all the time. But I'm not angry anymore. Not like I was. I know now I was born with a mother's heart. Perhaps not to be a mother, but to love like one. And maybe, just maybe, that's enough."

~ Danielle De Luca ~

We think about you always,
we talk about you still,
you have never been forgotten,
and you never will.
We hold you close within our hearts,
and there you will remain,
to walk with us throughout our lives
until we meet again.

~ Unknown

CHAPTER 5

Cooper Boudreau
Carson & Carter Boudreau
Scout Boudreau

September 21, 2004
June 16, 2007
October 28, 2008

Our story:

My husband and I met in 1995 and were married a year later. We were older and so were anxious to start a family. As the months went by and still no pregnancy I wasn't too concerned, as I was from a large family and had no reason to believe that there would be any problems. When we celebrated our 2nd anniversary and still no pregnancy, we decided to go and see our doctor. He ordered all sorts of tests and procedures. It was detected that both my husband and I were fine, and that there should be no reason for us not to be able to have a child. We spent the next several months using some fertility medications, in hopes to increase our chance of becoming pregnant. After that was unsuccessful, we spent a year undergoing six cycles of Intrauterine Inseminations (IUI's) along with fertility medications, and still no pregnancy. Along the way, we were prayerful, and both knew that children were in our future and that we would become parents. After that year of treatment, we were referred to a Reproductive Endocrinologist (RE) and it was decided that In-Vitro Fertilization (IVF) was the next step for us.

In 2001, and at the age of 39, my husband and I went through our first round of IVF. It was successful and after a very uneventful (but thrilling) pregnancy, I gave birth to our son Noah, on November 9th. He was beautiful, healthy and an absolute miracle. We knew if we wanted another biological child, we would need to go through another round of IVF. I was nearing my 40th birthday, so we knew time was an issue. Shortly after my birthday we completed our second round of IVF without success. We were disappointed, but also knew that with my age, we may need to do several rounds before a pregnancy would occur again. That being said, we went on for our third round and happily I became pregnant! We were thrilled and overcome with joy! At week seven, we returned to our RE for our first ultrasound, and were devastated when he was not able to find a heartbeat. He checked repeatedly and informed us of the sad news. I was frozen. I didn't know what to do. It had always been about getting pregnant for us, we had NEVER thought about anything happening once I became pregnant. The sadness was overwhelming!

After several months, we re-grouped and decided to return to our Dr. There was no explanation for our loss and due to my age at the time, we knew it was a long shot of becoming pregnant again. However, after meeting with our Dr. we continued and went through two more cycles of IVF, but both were unsuccessful. We decided we would make one more attempt and if it was not successful, we would move onto adoption. On our sixth attempt, I became pregnant and we were overjoyed, but also anxious! We went for our seven week ultrasound; panicked that again there would be no heartbeat. However, we were thrilled to see the flutter of a heartbeat and again we were overcome with happiness! Finally, after all of the unsuccessful attempts and the earlier loss, we would be able to have a second baby! My pregnancy had a few complications, but for the most part things were going well. On the morning of September 21st, 2004, I was getting ready for work, my husband had already left for work and my beautiful three year old son was sleeping in our bed. I used the restroom and felt a bulge protruding from my vagina. When I realized it was the amniotic sack, I panicked and tried to shove it back up inside of me and ruptured the sack with my fingernail. Fluid gushed everywhere and I sat frozen on the toilet. I was 42 years old, 17 weeks pregnant and my membranes had just ruptured. Trying not to wake my beautiful son, who was sleeping just a few feet away, I held in my hysteria and called my husband. I sat on the toilet for 30 minutes, while waiting for him to get home. We rushed to the hospital and met my OB-GYN there. They did an ultrasound to confirm the ruptured membranes. I remember lying on the table watching the screen and seeing an active baby with a strong heartbeat. I knew that by the end of the day our beautiful little baby would die. It was discovered that I was dilated 4 cm and that most likely the bulging membranes were due to an incompetent cervix. They induced labor, and for 12 hours my husband and I had time to prepare for the birth. That evening I delivered a baby boy, who we named Cooper. We had a wonderful nurse, who helped prepare us and made our time with him so precious and sacred. We will forever be grateful to her!

The grief was unbearable at times. I joined a support group and I got connected to an organization online. All were very helpful, but the desire for another baby was so powerful, that it made the grief even worse for me. I felt as though I needed to do something, so we decided to look into adoption. For the next two years we actively pursued adoption. We were connected with an agency and were also very active with friends and relatives in assisting us, with the hopes of connecting with a birth mother. Trying to adopt, actually helped with the grieving process. It gave me some hope that we could actually have another baby. We not only wanted another baby for ourselves, but for our son Noah. We did not want him to be alone and to be an only child. We wanted him to have a sibling, someone to go through this life with, especially after we were no longer here on the earth. However, at the end the two years and with no prospects, I felt the need to make a shift in our approach. Adoption had become a very passive process, which was very frustrating for me. The desire for another baby was all consuming. I'm sure others thought I had lost my mind!

After long talks with each other, we went back to our RE to discuss possible options. I was then 44 years old and knew using my own eggs would most likely not be a viable option. After meeting without Dr. we decided to use donor eggs, along with my husband's sperm and try IVF again. We knew the chances would be very high of getting pregnant and that if I did become pregnant, it would be considered High Risk, due to my prior loss. We discussed and strategized for the future, and we were excited and willing to take the risk. I became pregnant again and on my 45 birthday found out that I was carrying twins! Excited, thrilled, shocked and scarred, were the feelings I remember when we saw two sacks and two heartbeats. This of course complicated things especially with my cervical issues, but we had a plan. I saw my OB every week for monitoring, had a cerclage at 13 weeks, was put on modified bed rest at 16 weeks and finally was put on complete hospital bed rest at 18 weeks. Despite our plan, all of the precautions and the excellent medical care I received, our beautiful twin sons, Carson and Carter, were born on June 16, 2007, at 24 weeks and only survived a few hours. There are no words to express the complete despair we both felt. There was no support group, online or in person that was helpful to me. I felt as though a dark cloud consumed me and I could not shake it. I remember people saying, "Why can't you just be grateful for the son you have?" or "Well, at least you have one other child." All of which was not helpful! What was helpful to me was talking about the babies, looking at their photos, re-telling the story of what happened, ordering their headstone, visiting and grooming their grave with our son Noah, participating in local walk-a-thons to remember our babies, planting a tree in our back yard in memory for our four babies we had lost, ordering a piece of jewelry with their names on it and just being allowed to cry and grieve. For me it was not only the loss of our four babies, but it was the loss of a dream of completing our family. However, I was not finished!

Even after this devastating loss, we still had hope that there was another child for us, somehow. I couldn't share these feelings with most people, since I knew they thought I was crazy! My best friend said, "Haven't you been through enough?" My husband was very protective of me and although he had tried to "fix" me so that I wouldn't cry anymore and realized that was an impossible task for anyone, we had a serious "what now" conversation. My husband, so loving and so generous, was emotionally done and could not tolerate the idea of pursuing any more attempts to have a child, however, we both knew we still had frozen embryos from our last IVF cycle, and this weighed heavy on our hearts. We knew my body could not carry a baby to term and my mind was already racing with the idea of using a surrogate to carry a baby for us. With the help and encouragement of my family and our Dr., we decided to pursue surrogacy and were quickly connected to an agency. Within a few days we were connected with a wonderful woman, who became our surrogate. Our RE worked with us and our surrogate, who lived in another state. Two of our embryos were implanted and she became pregnant. We were so excited. I felt the dark cloud slightly lifting as we continued through the pregnancy. She had been a surrogate two previous times and had very successful and easy pregnancies. I was so anxious, but also felt that everything would work out. She was being followed by our Dr. and by her own OB near her home. Everything was going great! I was excited to participate in her 20 week check up/ultrasound via conference call. With past pregnancies we had always wanted to be surprised with the gender, but this time we decided we wanted to know. Our plan was that she was to call me from the office once she was prepped and ready to go. I was at work, in my office and anxiously awaited her phone call. I waited and I waited until I finally received her call. I could tell by the tone in her voice that something was wrong. My heart sunk as I heard the words, 'Lisa, I'm so, so sorry, the baby is dead." I couldn't breathe, everything went into slow motion. I told her I would need to call her back. I hung up the phone; got my things, told my boss I needed to leave, got in the car and drove home. I couldn't think about what I was just told, because I knew if I did I would fall apart and not be able to drive home. I arrived home, walked upstairs to my room, called my husband, laid down on our bed and began to sob. "How could this be happening to us again?" With all that we had been through, this was not fair! How could this have happened? Our precious baby girl, Scout, was stillborn on October 28, 2008. It was discovered that our surrogate had developed a slight blood clotting disorder during pregnancy, and it was believed that this caused a blood clot to travel through the cord to the baby. Once again I was back in a very dark place. The feelings that only a mother, who has lost a child, is familiar with. The feelings cannot even be put into words. We had been in touch with our surrogate, who we felt a true friendship and connection with, and reassured her that we in no way blamed her for the loss. She also was devastated by this loss, as she knew our history and was so happy to be helping us. A few days after the death of our baby girl, our surrogate called me. She told me that she and her husband had been talking and even though it may be a bit premature and too soon, she wanted us to know that she was willing to try another round of IVF. She truly wanted to help us. In the midst of my own grief, my mind again had been racing, thinking about the possibility of trying again, wondering if we could still use our current surrogate, even with the blood situation. So, when she said this to me, I was overjoyed and thrilled that she was so willing! Weeks later, we all talked with our RE and it was explained that if our surrogate took a daily injection of a blood thinner, we had an excellent chance of everything working out. We all decided to try IVF with our same surrogate again. So, in February of 2009 we started down the IVF road one last time. She became pregnant, and I was a nervous wreck from the beginning. Her Dr. saw her every other week, had multiple ultrasounds, continued with daily injections of a blood thinner and used a monitor at home to detect the fetal heartbeat. I was an emotional disaster throughout the entire pregnancy. She had a great and successful pregnancy and on November 10, 2009 she gave birth to our beautiful son Finnley. We were there for the birth and as we waited to go into the delivery room (she needed a C-section at the last minute) I looked at her OB and said, "I feel as though I have been holding my breath for 8 years, and now I can finally exhale!" Words cannot describe the joy we felt seeing and holding him for the first time. That first night in the hospital, it was just the three of us. While my husband held our miracle baby boy, he looked at me and said, "Thank you so much for not giving up on our dream!" Although the journey was a long one, with many pot holes along the way, it was all worth it in the end!

We are finally at peace knowing our family is now complete.

As a family we continue to remember our other babies who are not here with us on this earth; Cooper, Carson, Carter and Scout. We celebrate their birthdays, have a memory box for each of them, visit their grave, look at their photos and say their names. We honor them, we remember them and we love them. "Those we have held in our arms for a little while, we hold in our hearts forever."

~ Lisa Thompson-Boudreau ~

*for I will turn their mourning into joy,
and will comfort them,
and make them rejoice from their sorrow.*

Jeremiah 31:13

CHAPTER 6

Alfonso "Alfy" Anthony Vaccaro

April 6, 2012

My story:
It took me almost a full month to type Alfy's story.

Thursday, April 5, 2012, I had an appointment with my OB. I was 28 weeks pregnant. I remember going to work that day and being so excited for my afternoon appointment, for two reasons. 1) I couldn't wait to hear Alfy's (note that at this time we still referred to him as "the baby" because we did not know the sex) heartbeat again and to see how we were progressing. 2) We were doing staff interviews for our summer employees and the appointment meant we had to end interviews early that day. I love my job and even doing the interviews, but interviewing approximately 70 college students in the matter of 5 days can be a bit overwhelming and tiresome at times, especially when you are 28 weeks pregnant. I even missed an interview that afternoon due to a post office/lunch run with one of my hallway friends. Either way, I was excited for my appointment, to learn a little bit more about my kiddo.

I left work at approximately 3:15pm which was cutting it close for my 4:15pm appointment. (I commute approximately 45 miles each way and my OB's office is located 15 minutes past my house.) My husband and I drove separately that day to ensure that he would be on time to the appointment as well. I got to the office right at 4:15. We went in and waited for a couple of minutes as always. When called back, we went through the usual routine, put my purse in Room 8, step on the scale to see how the weight was coming (I hadn't put on any weight since my last appointment), pee in the cup, take blood pressure and answer some questions from the nurse.

The nurse asked me if I had been feeling movement from the baby. I told her I thought so but it was different than it was in the beginning. I had actually called the OB's office almost two weeks earlier (Monday, March 26) to inquire about the movement as it seemed to have changed. The nurse I spoke with told me that the feeling of movements generally change between 26 and 28 weeks due to the size of the baby, which is right where I was. I assumed the nurse had asked me about movement because there was a note in my chart reflecting this phone call.

My OB came in a few minutes later. I laid back on the table and she measured my stomach. She took out the fetal heart rate monitor and started to look for the Alfy's heartbeat, but she was having a hard time finding it. At this point I can say that I was not concerned. Alfy always had a way of moving during appointments that made him hard to see and/or hear. She suggested we do a quick ultrasound to check on him. We went to the ultrasound room just a few doors down. Even at this point, I still was not concerned. It had never crossed my mind that Alfy, my baby, my kiddo, might be gone.

The tech (a different one than we normally had) came in with my OB and they started the ultrasound. The monitor was turned away from me, but I could still glimpse a part of the screen. I only saw the blue color on the monitor, not the usual the red and blue that showed the pumping of blood. I looked at my OB and the tech. The tech was biting her lip and my OB told us that our baby no longer had a heartbeat. She said that he had been gone for a little while as he had some fluid built up in his abdomen, but she didn't know how long, just longer than 24 hours. I cannot begin to describe the feelings that passed through me at that moment. I looked at my husband and started crying. I started to recount the prior two weeks and asked her if I could have somehow prevented it. She told me no and that I had done nothing wrong. They left us alone for a little while. When they came back, my OB told me that due to Alfy's size I had to deliver him. She wanted to induce me that night and asked if we were comfortable going to a different hospital from the one we had planned on delivering at. She was required to be at that different hospital the following night because of the Easter holiday.

I'm not really sure how long that appointment took. I do know that it was past 5pm when we left because the waiting room was empty as were the hallways. Looking back I am thankful that I always made my appointments at the end of the day because I could not imagine running into another expecting mother during those moments. I drove home after the appointment and Tony went to exchange his work truck for his personal one, the one appointment we drove to separately.

When I got home I sat in my bathroom and cried. I started packing my bag for the hospital. We hadn't taken any birthing classes yet (we were registered for one the next weekend) so I had no idea what to pack. I decided that it didn't really matter all that much. I packed some comfy clothes and the essentials. Tony got home about 30 minutes after me, I think. (I don't really remember at this point.) We made the phone calls to our parents. We talked about names. We already knew the name if the baby was a boy and we picked out a girl name if the baby was a girl. The boy name was harder to discuss... the first born son in Tony's family is always named after his paternal grandfather, Alfonso Anthony. It was a little after 7 pm when we left the house.

Tony and I arrived at the hospital and were checked in by 7:45pm. We got our very own nurse. Her only responsibility was taking care of us for the night. At 9pm I was given a medicine to induce labor and had to lie in bed for 2 hours to allow it to take effect. I started cramping fairly soon after I received the medicine. I knew I was going to get an epidural, but I wanted to try and wait until my parents arrived (they had a 6 hour drive). I was hoping it would be close to midnight or 1am. I got the epidural at approximately 1:30am; my parents arrived at almost the same time. At 2:30am our parents came in and stayed until about 4:30am.

I don't really remember what was said during our parents' first visit or what I did during the down time that followed. I know there was lots of crying. In the hospital it was easier to be strong for our family. My water broke at about 10:30am. My parents were just getting to the hospital. I asked to see them for a few moments. Correction, I spoke with my mom and my water broke while my parents were in the room. I remember my dad saying it was a good thing they didn't take another 5 minutes, and it was. I had a new nurse at this point. She was so sweet, as was the OB resident. They called my regular OB, but she didn't make it to the hospital for the birth.

I was so scared of the delivery itself, but physically there was no pain, no pain at all. It took about 5 or 6 strong pushes and I delivered my baby. I looked at Tony and asked him if we had a boy. He started crying and I could tell by the look in his eye that we were the sad but proud parents of a little baby boy. Tony started shaking his head yes to confirm what I saw in his eyes. He cut the cord and I asked the doctor to lay Alfy on my chest. Earlier they had asked me if I wanted to hold him right away or if I wanted him to be wrapped up and have on his cap; I didn't have an answer for them at that moment. Once he was born, it was instinctual; I wanted to hold my son. It was 11:05am on Good Friday.

Some of the details have become a little fuzzy for me, so bear with me.

Tony and I spent some time with our son right after he was born, I don't remember how long. After Dr. Pearsall arrived they took Alfy for a little while to do his measurements, take footprints and handprints, inspect his little body, take some pictures and wrap him up. They brought him back and we spent at least a couple of hours with him. But eventually the focus was back on me.

My placenta did not want to deliver. We had been waiting patiently to see if it would come out on its own. It wouldn't. My doctor gave me a medicine to help loosen it from my uterine wall. It didn't work. She gave me another medicine, it didn't work. She gave me a third medicine, one with absolutely horrendous side effects. She tried massaging and pushing on my stomach to loosen it and get it to come out. It didn't work. She said there was the option of heading to an OR or waiting a little bit longer. It had been several, miserable hours. I opted for the OR.

I don't know what time I went down there. Tony might remember. I hate that I had to leave him alone. I was given medicine through my IV to "take the edge off." My doctor tried to force out my placenta. Again, I don't know how long she tried. It didn't work. They put me under and surgically removed my placenta. I don't know how long this took.

I woke up in the recovery room receiving a blood transfusion. Once I was awake and alert they wheeled me back to my room on the L&D floor. I was so happy to see Tony again. I believe it was close to 5pm now. At this point we had not talked to our parents since we told them my water had broken. We gave it a little bit of time. We had the nurse bring Alfy back to us. Tony went and got our parents. We all held him and the nurse took pictures for us. I was shaking so bad I was afraid to hold him, afraid I would hurt his little body. Tony helped me. We held him together. The hospital chaplain came and did a blessing for us.

Eventually we had to give him back to the nurses and send him down to the morgue. Room temperature air was hard on his little body and we wanted to baptize him the next day, after our siblings arrived. The nurse told us that he wouldn't be alone in the morgue; there were other babies and people down there to be his friends. What a sad but somewhat comforting thought.

For what seems like the millionth time I've said it, I don't remember the rest of the evening all that well. I took an Ambien around 11 and remember seeing the clock at 11:20pm. The next thing I remember is waking up crying. I had heard the word "Mommy" right before waking up. Tony climbed in bed with me. A little while later I was supposed to try to get out of bed (they had taken the epidural out after surgery some time). I got my legs off the side of the bed and almost passed out.

I received another blood transfusion that morning. It started at 8am and finished at noon shortly after our parents came in to sit with us. It was now Saturday, April 7.

The baptism was scheduled for 2pm, which was a good thing as my brother, my sister, my soon-to-be brother-in-law and almost-3-month-old my nephew arrived around 1:30pm. Tony's sister had gotten there earlier that day. They are all Alfy's Godparents. The hospital chaplain was late. Alfy arrived in our room right around 2pm. Our nurse that day had never had to work with a family that had a child that was born still. She was a postpartum nurse and had been sent down to take care of me. She was so genuine, not that the other nurses weren't, but there was a sadness she shared with us. I will never forget her or any of the other nurses. She asked Tony to come see Alfy before she brought him in to make sure everything was right.

At about 2:30pm, the chaplain arrived and we did the baptism. It was beautiful. After the baptism, Tony and I had to say goodbye to our son, to our Alfy. I believe that was the saddest moment in my life, knowing I would never see my son again.

I left the hospital at 7pm that evening, almost 48 hours after I had arrived. Our nurse took us down through the back stairwell by our room. Tony took the stairwell by himself first to get the truck and park it by the exit for me. He had to walk back up through the L&D floor. He rode an elevator with another new dad that told him "Congratulations." Tony told him our son was born still. He told Tony he was sorry and gave him a hug in the elevator. I wish Tony didn't have to experience walking back through the L&D floor by himself. We left the hospital, with no baby in tow. We spent the rest of the evening with our family, our wonderful, loving, supportive family.

Sunday was Easter. Our family came over in the afternoon to be with us. Tony's parents brought pasta so we didn't have to cook. Before everyone came, Tony and I went to Babies 'R Us to buy Alfy clothing to be buried in. We didn't have any baby clothes yet. We bought him a preemie onesie, but I'm certain it was still way too big for his little body. It was white, with a baby blue color and cuffs on the arms. It had zoo animals on it, giraffes, tigers, lions and elephants and it had feet in it. I tried to find a cap that I thought would fit, but they didn't have any that would. Seriously?! And it was the only place open on Easter other than Wal-Mart to buy baby clothes.

Monday we went to the funeral home at 9am. We decided what time Alfy's funeral would be and made all the arrangements. We had to view the tiny caskets they make for babies. Alfy's casket was 19 inches long, that's it, 19 inches. It was white with some gray in it. The funeral home called St. Cecilia's for us to ask Father Gutsgell to come and pray for Alfy and help lay our son to rest. He was the priest who married Tony and me. Although I am not Catholic, Father Gutsgell has been there for me for spiritual guidance on two of the most important days of my life. After the funeral home we had to go to the cemetery to pick out the location we would lay our child to rest, and will eventually lie in rest ourselves. It's a beautiful spot. It's just to the west of a giant tree (I don't remember what kind right now) and almost to the bottom of a hill.

On Tuesday, April 10, at 1:30pm, Tony and I buried our son, Alfy.

This is not the end of Alfy's story, just the end of the beginning for him. He will continue to move me in ways I never knew possible and that is how his story will go on.

The hardest part for me:
The hardest part was losing my child, hands down. I will forever be the parent of a child who is dead. That is some heavy stuff that most people don't go through. The second hardest part, which I believe is important to mention is the loss/changes of what were once reliable and steady relationships. The people I had counted the most on in my life up until the point of losing Alfy were the ones who caused the most damage after Alfy died, with the exception of my husband. My family, closest family, and my friends, best friends, were nowhere to be found. Not only do you go through the grieving process for your own child, which is nearly impossible, but you also grieve the relationships that were once important to you. Through some work and forgiveness I've made some steps in repairing a few of them, but they will never be quite the same.

Helpful things from family and friends:
I had one friend, Nic, who wasn't afraid of me and my grief. She drove 8 hours the day before Alfy's funeral, just to give me a hug. Nic was the first person to ask me about Alfy, about his delivery, about all the details. She never stopped being my friend or being afraid of me. I don't know if she'll ever know how important her friendship is to me. I am proud to say that Nic is now the godmother of our second son.

Speak my child's name. Recognize that my child existed and that my pain is real. Cry with me. Don't say something just for the sake of saying something, especially to justify the loss. There is no justification for losing a child. It was not part of God's plan. Everything does not happen for a reason. God does give me more than I can handle.

Things that have helped me cope and deal with the heartache:
My husband, impatiently patient husband, Tony, my pets (Desda our dog and Piper our cat), my second son, Vinny and his infectious smiles, my thoughtful and open grief counselor, Hannah.

I have learned:
We shouldn't be afraid to speak of death. Speaking of death and those that have died is a reminder that our loved ones were once alive and very important to us.

How I keep my baby's memory alive:
Alfy is part of his brother's life. We celebrate his birthday, include him during holidays and always make his presence known in our house. My husband, Tony, made Alfy his own toy box that sits in our living room. The box contains all of our most precious things that belonged to Alfy and the things that have been done to remember him. Remembering him doesn't always happen the same way each year either. I have to work at it. I will admit, at this point in my journey I long to do more, I just don't know what at this point. I'm hoping to find it soon.

Additional words:
If you are reading this because of your own loss, I am so sorry. Know that you are not alone in your journey.

~Shannon Vaccaro~

The Cord

We are connected, my child and I,
By an invisible cord, not seen by the eye.

It's not like the cord that connects us 'til birth
This cord can't be seen by any on earth.

This cord does its work right from the start.
It binds us together, attached to my heart.

I know that it's there though no one can see
The invisible cord from my child to me.

The strength of this cord man couldn't create.
It withstands the test, can hold any weight.

And though you are gone,
Though you're not here with me,
The cord is still there, but no one can see.

It pulls at my heart. I am bruised... I am sore,
But this cord is my lifeline as never before.

I am thankful that God
Connects us this way
A mother and child
Death can't take away.

~ Unknown

CHAPTER 7

Samuel Brian Mackey

January 27, 2013 – April 14, 2013
11 weeks / 77 days

My story:
The Beginning- Samuel's Birth

Samuel Brian Mackey is my husband, John's, and mine first child. He is now our angel baby.

Samuel brought me many happy days in his short life. The positive pregnancy test was the first day. The morning of Thursday August 30, 2012 is when we found out we were pregnant. My husband and I were thrilled. A rush of emotions surged through me over the next few days- shock, excitement, happiness, joy, wonderment; I was on a natural high.

Our baby was due on April 30, 2013. My pregnancy was progressing as it should, and baby was growing on schedule. My baby did its most active kicking at night. Once I was settled and comfortable in bed, baby would start dancing across my belly! The night of Wednesday January 23, 2013, baby did no such movements. I wasn't concerned until I woke up the next morning and still did not feel baby move. I knew something wasn't right. I went into the doctor's office to listen to baby's heartbeat. The heartbeat was there, but so were contractions. I did not feel those contractions at all, but they were causing baby's heart rate to drop. We then proceeded with an ultrasound to check my amniotic fluid level. That was normal. At this point my husband and I still did not know the sex of our baby. So I cheated and found out during the ultrasound. "It's a boy!" I cannot even describe the joy I felt hearing those words. I wanted a boy so badly. We were having a "Samuel." My wish came true.

After the ultrasound I was in a room waiting for the doctor to do a vaginal exam. She wasn't down there very long and I didn't feel her do much, but the first words out of her mouth were, "Oh my God! This is bad." Then she mumbled something about a c-section. She said my cervix was bulging and I was 2-3cm dilated. At that moment my heart shattered into a million pieces. The first words out of my mouth were, "I just want him to live." I had read that babies can survive at 26 weeks out of the womb. I was crying. I was hysterical. I was shaking. I was in shock. What did this mean? Would my baby survive? My entire life was just flipped upside down. I called my husband and my parents to come to the hospital. In the meantime, I was taken to Labor & Delivery.

Basically, the plan was strict bed rest and medications to lighten contractions. I was inverted in bed for a day and a half. I had a hard time giving up the life I was used to and had a lot of thoughts going through my head during that time. I had to come to terms that this was happening and that being in the hospital was the best thing for my son.

Saturday showed improvement. The nurse checked my cervix and it was now thicker and higher up. I was able to get off the magnesium, which was causing weird images in my head. My bed was able to be flat. I was unhooked from all monitors and lines and only on the baby monitor intermittently. I was able to walk to the bathroom, but still on bed rest. I was able to be in my own clothes. I was able to eat anything!

Not much went on Sunday morning. I can't believe how fast the time went by when all I did was stare blankly at the TV screen. That afternoon, around 3p my water broke. Half an hour later I started having back contractions, which then moved to the front of my belly. With my amniotic fluid level now significantly lower, the contractions were putting more stress on Samuel. He was able to tolerate the contractions for a few hours. When the doctor didn't like what she was seeing on the monitor anymore, she came in and said. "It's time to get that baby out." I delivered Samuel by c-section at 6:35p on Sunday January 27, 2013. He was 2 pounds, 9 ounces and 13.5 inches. I was not conscious during my son's birth because the spinal block did not work and they had to put me under because I was hysterical being without my husband. Samuel was rushed to the NICU; my husband only able to catch a glimpse of him.

I did not meet my son until the following afternoon. On the way to the NICU, I was so excited and nervous. My heart was racing. I was giddy and felt a huge smile on my face. I wondered if my son would even like me. The moment I laid eyes on Samuel, I fell in love with him. My heart grew a hundred times its size in that moment. I loved everything about him, his dark hair, his hands and feet, the fuzzy hair on his body. He looked just like me! Our son is here! We have a baby now!

It hurt me to see my son in an incubator, attached to so many tubes and wires. I hated my body for kicking him out so early. We later learned that going into premature labor was caused by an intrauterine infection.

The Middle- Our NICU Normal

Tuesday night, January 29, was magical because that was the first time Samuel and I kangarooed. I took my shirt off and the nurse placed him on my chest and wrapped us in warm blankets. That was the first time I felt like a mommy. I loved holding him. It made me so happy and content. On Wednesday I was discharged from the hospital. It was so hard to leave Samuel. I was in tears as we drove away. But we came back for his 9p assessment so I could hold him again. During that time I also took his temperature and changed his diaper. We spent two hours there because I also pumped at his bedside after I held him.

My husband works a lot, 12-14 hours a day. He works hard to provide for his family and so I could be a stay at home mom. He was only able to visit Samuel once or twice a week. Samuel and John had a strong connection even while Samuel was in my womb. That bond continued, separated by the glass of the incubator. Samuel always looked his daddy in the eyes when he heard his voice; a gesture of love between a father and son.

I visited Samuel every single day during one of his assessment times. There was so much medical jargon to try and understand about the health of our baby. John was better at processing and understanding it than I was. I was just focused on doing Samuel's cares and giving him my unconditional love.

You know how you go through your whole life searching…for meaning, for purpose, for direction, guidance, answers? My entire life made sense to me when I held my son for the first time. It's like everything just fell into place, perfectly. The puzzle was complete. Samuel was the missing piece. Samuel completed me. He completed John and me. My life continued to make sense every time he was in my arms. The chemistry between us when we were skin to skin was electrifying. I could feel the love flow between us and through my veins.

As humans we are creatures of habit, we like routine. At least I do. I developed a routine with Samuel. During the days, I was home pumping every three hours, he received my breast milk through a feeding tube. I spent most of my days preparing the house for his arrival and preparing myself mentally as well. But when 5p came and I was at the hospital with my son, nothing else mattered. The outside world faded away and it seemed like Samuel and I were the only two people on earth.

"Hi Samuel, Mommy's here. I love you!" This is how I greeted my son every day. The nurse would come over and give me an update as to how he was doing and where his oxygen levels were at. Then I would begin his cares. I started with taking his temperature, sometimes he would fuss because I had to lift his arm up. He'd make a squishy face and stick his tongue out, but I couldn't hear him cry because the ventilator tube went through his vocal chords. Next, I changed his diaper. I loved changing Samuel's diaper. I wanted to make sure he was urinating and stooling normally. He always did. I'd go wash my hands and come back to do eye and mouth care. I used saline wipes for his eyes and nursery water and a swab for his mouth. I put Aquaphor on his lips so they wouldn't dry out. Then we would kangaroo for one hour during his feeding. Later on, that hour turned into an hour and half because I loved holding Samuel, I loved taking naps with my son. I held him until my bottom was numb from being in the recliner. When Samuel was in my arms I sang to him, I told him about my day, I read to him. He was the best part of my day. He made me so happy. He took my outside of myself.

Once he was settled back into his incubator, I pumped. After I put my milk in the freezer and cleaned my supplies, I sat at Samuel's bedside and talked to or read or sang to him some more. I was there for three hours each night, from 5-8p. It was hard to say goodnight, hard to leave him in the NICU and go home without him. I told him how much I loved him. "Goodnight Samuel. Sweet dreams. I love you my son. I love you sweet boy. I love you! I love you! I love you!"

The first thing they tell you in the NICU is that there will be a rollercoaster of ups and downs that Samuel will go through. He received his first of several blood transfusions throughout his life on February 3 because his hemoglobin level was low. On February 7, Samuel was put on the ventilator because he was having apnea spells and they had to keep raising his oxygen levels. He had pneumonia in the beginning of March. He had a heart murmur since birth which did not close in its own, so he had to have a PDA ligation done on March 12. He did move into an open crib on March 19 because he could regulate his own body temperature. This made it easier to give him lots of kisses!

Samuel developed a left inguinal hernia. This means his intestines descended into his scrotum. He would have needed surgery to correct this before he came home. He had a yeast infection on his groin because his fragile skin had poor ability to fight off germs, but that went away with the application of topical ointment. Samuel had several eye exams showing he had early Retinopathy of Prematurity, abnormal growth of blood vessels in the retina. This was being monitored weekly.

Samuel was showing improvement towards the end of March. His nurses were able to gradually wean his oxygen rate down to 14%!!! It was looking hopeful that we were soon going to get him off that ventilator. On March 31 Samuel had a fever of 103°. This was because the pneumonia had returned. His blood was also infected with a Staphylococcus aureus and Enterococcus feacalis. Looking back this was probably Samuel's threshold; all that his little, underdeveloped body could handle.

The End- Samuel's Death

On March 25 and March 30, Samuel coded. His heart rate and oxygen levels dropped significantly, but they were able to bring him back. There was also another time, on April 2, when I was holding him that he froze in my arms. I thought I had lost him then. But he came back to me.

I thought Saturday April 13, 2013 was going to be another routine day visiting my son. At 5:30p, after his cares, Samuel and I were skin to skin. His nurse and I were talking about creating a plan with his doctors to get him home sooner. She took a couple pictures of Samuel, and then let us be together. At 6p, Jennifer, Samuel's aunt and Godmother, came for a visit. We had a nice, sisterly chat until 7p when she had to leave. While conversing with Jennifer, my attention was on Samuel. I was feeling the joy in holding him and being his mommy; I envisioned our future together. He did so well while I was holding him. His oxygen saturation never fell below 88. The nurse didn't have to come in at all to adjust his levels. Shortly after Jennifer left, I decided to put Samuel back in his crib. I was going to read or sing to him once he was settled, then pump. His nurse picked him up from my chest and placed him back in his crib. While she was hooking Samuel back up, I put my shoes back on and fixed my shirt. I noticed he was crying and upset, so I walked around to the other side of the crib to comfort him. I put my hand on his head and said, "Don't cry Samuel." Then he froze and stopped breathing. More and more nurses surrounded him, I moved out of the way. I wasn't even worried since he's done this before; I thought they would bring him back. I felt like an observer. I felt like I was watching "E.R." or "Grey's Anatomy." This was not happening. Dr. C came in. He looked nervous, frantic even. He took out Samuel's vent tube and put a new one in. He wanted me to leave the room, but I wouldn't. I needed to be there, for Samuel and as a witness for my own piece of mind. I couldn't see anything though; too many people were blocking the sight of my son. I still wasn't worried yet. I thought they would bring him back. At this point they kicked me all the way out of the room. I didn't know what was going on or what to make of the situation. Dr. C came out twice and told me each time that this isn't good and that he doesn't think Samuel is going to make it. I told him to keep trying. They were giving him Epinephrine to jump start his heart and doing chest compressions. Samuel was not responding well to these measures. It took forty minutes to get Samuel "stable" and a heart rate established. When I was able to see my son, his body was lifeless, he looked fake. I knew to check his eyes. They were frozen in place and glazed over; the look of death. I burst out crying. I tried calling him back to me while I shook his little hand, "Samuel... Samuel..." I knew my son wasn't there anymore; they were just keeping his body alive. I stepped out to call John and my parents. When I came back he was on a different machine, an oscillator. It was shaking his little body constantly to oxygenate his blood; it was doing his breathing for him 100%. His nurse was listening to his heart with her stethoscope; I asked if I could listen too. I heard a very faint heartbeat being drained out by the noise of the oscillator. That was my glimmer of hope. His heart was still beating...

Samuel stayed on that machine all night, into the following morning. It was then when his heart rate started to drop. He was given Epinephrine which brought it back up. An x-ray that was done showed he had an enlarged heart and that his intestines were getting bigger. Samuel's stomach was expanding before our eyes. His nurses prepared us for what could happen and we had Samuel baptized by the hospital chaplain. John, myself, and my mom sat by Samuel's bedside. I started reading to him just so he could hear my voice. John continued to hold his hand. At 8:27a Samuel's heart rate dropped below 80 bpm. I looked at the monitor and read 75 bpm. We moved to make way for the team. His heart rate dropped to 50. They started compressions and Epinephrine, they were not working. His heart rate continued to drop...into the 30's...teens...down to zero in six minutes. At 8:33a Samuel's heart stopped. I listened with the stethoscope;

I heard nothing, just an empty body cavity. But we had them continue with CPR while the chaplain said a prayer. When he was done the doctors said there was nothing else they could do. I listened again for his heart beat, but there was nothing. I looked up at John and saw his tears. We gave them the ok to stop. At 8:53a Samuel died. I picked up my son and hugged and kissed him. They disconnected his wires and tubes and handed him to me. That was the first time I saw my son's face without tape and tubes; it was the first time I held my son like a mother holds her baby.

The hardest part for me:
There are a few moments that stand out as being the most difficult. One was leaving the hospital for the last time without my baby. To walk out of the hospital doors knowing that I didn't have to come back was surreal, so out of the ordinary since it was my routine. I went to the hospital everyday for two and a half months to take care of my son. That was like his temporary home to me.

Never being able to put my son to my breast and breastfeed him broke my heart. I was very disciplined in pumping every three hours to keep my supply up for Samuel. I even had fits and yelled at my husband if we were away from home for longer than that. I had to get home and pump for my son! After Sam died, when the lactation nurse came in and told me ways to ease off of pumping to let my milk dry up, I exploded with tears. An initiation into motherhood that Sam and I will never experience together.

I had a freezer and half of a deep freezer full of the breast milk that I pumped for Samuel. It hurt me to part with it thinking maybe a miracle would happen and he would need it someday, but I was able to donate it to a mother who adopted a baby that could only tolerate breast milk. I was thankful that it was used for a good cause.

What I still struggle with on a daily basis is that I still get to continue living my life when Samuel's ended so soon. It plagues my mind with questions about the meaning of life, wondering if it will make any sense. If I could just understand a tiny piece of it, I would feel better.

I would willingly trade places with Samuel so he could experience and feel all that life has to offer. I was supposed to watch my son grow up and teach him how to read and write and be the best version of himself. Instead, our roles have reversed and he is the one teaching me now.

Helpful things from family and friends:

I have to give the most credit to my husband, especially because he arranged Samuel's funeral. I was in no state mentally or emotionally to make those decisions. John took charge from the start in finding a funeral home that would honor our wishes. I am very proud of him as my husband and Samuel's father.

My family was remarkable in helping with all the details of Samuel's funeral. They had less than two days to get everything prepared. My brother put together a beautiful photo montage using all the photos I took of Samuel; seeing the pictures flow from one to the next really showed Samuel's journey in the NICU. My mom, sister, and sister-in-law made precious bookmarks with Sam's photo and a heart touching poem. They also scurried to make a display of Samuel's photos in matching frames for the front. My friend Deanna and my cousins helped out by bringing snacks for guests to munch on until the service began.

It meant a lot to us that in a time of need our families were there for us to honor our son and say goodbye to his body.

Things that have helped me cope and deal with the heartache:
Looking back, the first few months after Samuel died, I was completely numb. But that numbness allowed me to be a mommy to my son. I worked on so many projects for him. I put every good picture I have of him in frames around my house. I read grief books, I journaled, I took pictures for Carly Marie's Grief Project, I went to support groups, I put together care packages for other grieving moms, I wrote articles and poems to express my grief, and I developed a brief interest in photography and went on photo shoots to explore the details of nature. Gradually the numbness faded and I was left to face the harsh reality of continuing to live my life without Samuel. There is an underlying pain in each of my days. Time lessens the pain, but it also takes me further away from remembering what Samuel felt like.

There are moments I look back and can't believe those few short months even happened. But my tears and the ache in my heart prove to me that it did. I learned that in order to keep on keeping on, I have to find things that motivate me, distract me, so I can live and grieve simultaneously. Life is all about balance.

No matter how silly or extreme it may seem to others, find things about your baby to hold onto that make you smile and remember your baby with joy. Whether it is a belief, song, sign, rainbow, butterfly, etc. For me, it is a pair of doves and cardinals that visit my balcony, always at the right moment. I'll be having a sad moment when I get the urge to lift my head and there they are. I always say, "Hi Samuel. I love you!"

I have learned:
The death of my son is the most difficult journey of my life. And it is a journey that I will travel until Samuel and I can be together again. Because the love I have for my son goes so deeply into my soul, the grief goes just as deeply. I hurt, I ache, I feel like my soul is missing. Grief takes a lot of time and effort to understand and process. It has many layers and is draining and exhausting. It's challenging to be strong all the time and want to make my son proud of me. It's easy to get sucked into the gloom and darkness. There are many days that I battle with choosing between light and dark. Some days I do choose dark because I just need to get through it to see the light on the other side.

Samuel walks beside me now; guiding me, inspiring me, teaching me valuable life lessons that I should have spent my life teaching him. Our babies know all too well that life is short and our days are numbered. We must find joy and happiness every day. We must love and live and not get bogged down with the mundane.

How I keep my baby's memory alive:
I attend memorial events hosted by local support groups. I want the world to know that Samuel lived, that his life is still important, no matter how short, no matter that only his family knew and loved him. It's bittersweet to hear his name read aloud at the ceremonies, it seems that's the only way I am able to hear it.

Additional Words:
Words of Wisdom

Each and every one of us travels the road of grief differently. It took me several months to chisel away the stone that encased my heart to find that underneath the grief, heartache, pain, and sorrow…there is love. A love as deep and intense as the grief itself. After all, aren't grief and love the same thing? They are the same road that do not end and go on forever. It's difficult to envision yourself traveling to that point when the fog is so dense and you're so focused on what was taken from you. But when the intensity of the sadness lifts you'll find there is love and joy and hope and gratitude. This is what unites us and brings us together…the infinite love we have for our babies.

Our babies' were a gift to us that we had to give back too soon. We are our babies' legacies. We are the ones still here to be their voices, to make them known to the world, and to be the best parents we can be to their precious souls. They shaped us into the people we are today. The best gift we could give to them is to live our lives with mindfulness and intention. Letting every thought, decision, and action come from the place of love where our babies' reside in our hearts.

~ Teresa Mackey ~

I waited patiently for the LORD;
and he inclined unto me,
and heard my cry.

Psalms 40:1

CHAPTER 8

Two Angels

2004 & 2005

My Story:
Pregnancy loss #1...

I was a starry eyed 25 year old. Just freshly moved to Las Vegas, Nevada to be with my now husband. While I was well travelled, I hadn't lived out of the Columbus/Cincinnati-area my whole life. I met a young guy about 2 years older than me who was also raised in Ohio. I was on vacation in Vegas, and he had just left Ohio to move out west. At the time, the town and jobs were booming and that's where everyone was going. We got engaged, and our wedding date was set for 10 months later. A month before our wedding I was on the positive end of a pregnancy test. I went to the doctor, who sees nothing wrong, and starts me on prenatal vitamins. About a week later I started bleeding heavily and my fiancé rushed me to the hospital, where we proceed to get stuck in a closet. It literally was an extra room because we were told it was "Fight Night" in Sin City and no one knew what to do with me...it was horrible. They didn't even perform an ultrasound; a doctor came in once to check on me, I was discharged, and I miscarried by the end of the week. We were told "at least you can get pregnant"...and were left to deal with the emotional mess afterwards with no guidance whatsoever. Forget my OBGYN...nowhere to be found after this.

All this one month before I was set to get married.

Pregnancy loss #2

A little over a year after our first miscarriage, I had switched OBs. It was Thanksgiving weekend. Repeat of scenario #1, except different hospital, but at least they did an ultrasound to confirm what was going on. I still received the same after-care though, and heard the same words again..."At least you can get pregnant." My OB wanted to hand us over to the fertility specialists, but seeing me and my now husband weren't even 30, we decided against it. This was now my second pregnancy loss in 2 years. This was November 2005.

Oh really? I can get pregnant?

Fast forward to December 2009; my career is on the fast track, and my husband and I had decided that maybe kids just weren't in the cards for us. We bought a new house...things were rolling. We were planning to go to

Palm Springs for a New Years Eve bash. Long story short; no pregnancies...not one until the pregnancy test that my husband insisted I take came up positive in December 2009. Given our history, I was apprehensive. Two months later, an ultrasound confirmed a healthy baby, now a beautiful young girl. And that young girl has a baby brother nearly 2 years younger than her (almost to the day).

No one was ever able to explain to us why we lost our first two, and then go on to have two very healthy pregnancies, but I still think about what my first two children would've looked like or been like. And my first successful pregnancy was so difficult emotionally; I was forever waiting for something to go wrong that I couldn't enjoy it.

Words can't explain all the emotional upheaval during the first two losses, and then now, there is nothing to say other than I'll see the first two on the other side, someday...

~ Becky Gauthier~

Fingerprints

Your fingerprints are on my heart.
Even though you never held my hand
You touched me.
Even though I never heard you speak
You taught me.
You taught me about love.
You taught me about caring.
You taught me about courage.
You taught me about faith.
You taught me about happiness.
You taught me about sorrow.
You brought me closer to myself.
In the time I cared for you,
How my life changed.
Never to be the same again.
Because of you
I know I will somehow be stronger.
Because of you
I know I will be more prepared for life.
All this from tiny fingerprints
That touched my heart.
Because of this
You will live forever in my soul
Never to be forgotten.
I will always love you.
You are my child.

Born still but still born.

~Unknown

CHAPTER 9

Lucia Anne Massenzio

July 4, 2013 – September 20, 2013

Our story:
My husband and I were so excited to have a baby girl! We have an amazing 3 year old son and couldn't wait for him to be a big brother! My pregnancy was progressing normally, which was an immense relief at the time. I experienced a loss the first time we tried to start our family and our son was born prematurely at 31 weeks. So we were thrilled to hear all of the doctor reports that our baby girl was developing and growing just as she was "supposed" to be. Then everything changed early in the morning on July 4th when I was just 27 weeks.

I awoke in the middle of the night and was very uncomfortable. After getting up several times, I called the doctor who told us to go to the emergency room/ PET unit at the hospital. My husband, our son, and I rushed to the hospital. As soon as I got there, the team of doctors and nurses recognized that our baby was in distress (fetal bradycardia) and I was immediately taken in for an emergency c-section. I think my bed literally screeched around the corners as the team ran me down the hall and into the operating room. Everything was happening so quickly around me, it was clear that something was going very wrong.

Our daughter's birth was extremely traumatic for both of us as I suffered from a placental abruption. She lost oxygen and needed resuscitation. Though she came off the ventilator within about a day, she was still extremely premature and requiring a lot of support in the NICU. She was adorable still and we were immediately in love. Our baby girl had arrived and we named her Lucia.

Since we had gotten familiar with the NICU with our son, we thought that our experience would be similar, though we expected it to be tougher for Lucia since she was so much earlier than our son. After about 3 weeks in the NICU everything seemed to change. Lucia experienced her first seizure late one night and that was when we started to learn more about the severity of her brain injury from her birth. She had EEG and MRI testing and shortly thereafter she was diagnosed with hypoxic ischemic encephalopathy (HIE) when she was just 4 weeks old. We remained hopeful, though the more we talked to the doctors, researched day and night, and watched our daughter struggle with some of the basics; we were also experiencing the most frightening time of our lives. But we kept going. Our love for Lucia was growing by the minute and we were trying to do everything we could to help our baby girl. We held her as much as we could, talked to her, helped with her physical therapy, played classical music in her crib...and when she would open her eyes and look at us our hearts would melt.

Lucia remained in the NICU of the hospital where she was born for almost two months, but we were growing impatient with the doctors and truly didn't feel confident that she was getting the neurological attention that she needed. So we made the decision to seek more specialized opinions and moved her to a Children's Hospital that was a couple hours away. Once we arrived, the neurologists and neonatologists confirmed our greatest fears for our daughter. Her brain injury was severe and it was showing in her entire body. She was never able to suck or swallow, experienced countless apnea and bradycardia episodes, and didn't seem to be getting any better as she got closer to "term".

Our precious daughter's life was nearing the end and we had to try to prepare ourselves for what would be the most difficult day of our lives. We brought our son to visit with her and had the most precious day. He got the chance to be a big brother and we were even more proud of him than we expected to be. He kissed her, talked to her, and even got to play doctor with her in her crib and we spent the day just the four of us. We also were able to have both sets of Lucia's grandparents visit and had her baptized. We wanted our girl to know how much she was loved and I hoped and prayed every minute that she felt that love all around her.

On Friday September 20th, my husband and I held Lucia in our arms as she went to heaven. She was only two and a half months old.

Losing Lucia has left such a hole in our hearts, our arms and our life. Not a day goes by that we don't think about our daughter and wish that our experience had been different. Many days still I cry in bed at night, at work, and at times when I least expect it. I continue to work through the grief and struggle with my faith now more than ever, but I try to honor my daughter by being a little more patient. By trying to savor the everyday moments with my son for he is growing up so fast, my husband, my family and friends because those times are what truly matters. And I try to take the stressful and busy days in stride.

We received many conflicting opinions from Lucia's doctors and we got our hopes up for awhile during her short life only to have them shattered once we were able to have more experienced and specialized doctors see her. There are many parents who have children with HIE and their lives are both rewarding and extremely difficult. Maybe we can help some parents with our story. Much of the "loss" support that is available is specific to miscarriage and stillbirth, but not as much related to the loss of an infant, particularly after 2 ½ months time. It is the most horrible thing that we can experience and we will never have an answer to why this happened to any of us.

The hardest part for me:

We were very lucky in that we got to know our daughter for 2 ½ months. I held her almost every day, got to change her diaper, take her temperature, do physical therapy exercises with her, and even dress her once she moved to a crib. When she looked at me it felt amazing. We fell in love with her and had immense hope that her brain injury wouldn't be "that bad" and that she could still grow to be a happy, healthy, beautiful little girl. While it's a blessing that we got to know her, it's also the most difficult part because I think it's made it harder to let her go. All I want to do is remember the way she felt in my arms and I'm terrified that as time goes on those memories will fade. The other thing that is so difficult is that our 3 year old son was looking forward to having a little sister and while he knows she's gone, he still longs to have a baby sister. It breaks our hearts that he had one and then she was taken away from all of us.

Helpful things from family and friends:

The supportive phone calls, cards and visits were helpful and just knowing that people care. It's still extremely isolating though. Even friends, who have experienced the loss of a miscarriage or even the loss of infant due to stillbirth, don't understand since everyone's experience is so different. It makes me feel good when people ask about Lucia now that some time has passed or want to talk with me about what happened. Some people don't want to bring it up and avoid the topic altogether, but I don't mind talking about it to friends, family, or colleagues who are interested and my husband and I both really appreciate it when they ask. I've read other parents say that it makes them feel as though their child was here and mattered, and that is absolutely true.

Things that have helped me cope and deal with the heartache:
It makes me feel better to look through her pictures. In the week after she died, I made a photo book which was helpful for me and I treasure it now. It's also been helpful to read quotes on infant loss and think about her as an angel in heaven. But I think most of all, when those moments of heartache and grief come over me, I just have to feel it, talk about it, or cry.

I have learned:
I learned to be more "in the moment" from Lucia and I try to remind myself of this often. I cherish every moment I had with her and have thought that maybe she taught me to be better and savor the moments that I have with my son. Also, always fight for answers from your doctors. Never accept something if you don't feel in your heart that it is accurate or that you could learn more. It's easy to say "trust your gut" but it's another to act on that instinct.

How I keep my baby's memory alive:
I continue to think about her and look at her pictures. We are also considering how to honor her for the anniversary of her death - balloon release, visit to cemetery,

etc. My husband and I are also considering more ways we can honor her memory in the form of a foundation or other avenues that could help parents through a difficult time such as we had.

~ Melanie Massenzio ~

While we look not at the things which are seen, but at the things which are not seen: for the things which are seen are temporal; but the things which are not seen are eternal.

2 Corinthians 4:18

 CHAPTER 10

Eden Rose Gidwitz Santi

February 19, 2003
(She lived for 3.33 minutes)

My story:
I got pregnant on my first try. And I loved being pregnant.

I went to hospital to be induced on the 19th. Induced, dilated, baby's head would not engage in birth canal so opted for a "C" section.

After Eden was delivered, I asked? "Why isn't she crying?" Nurses said "It's ok, some baby's do not cry. We are taking her to neo-natal intensive care." I was taken up to recovery and shortly after, a doctor came in and said "There is something seriously wrong with your baby, it could be one of 3 things... we are rushing her over to Children's Memorial, would you like to see her before we go?"

They wheeled me down in the gurney into a room where 30 hospital nurses, medical staff, etc. were standing over a big incubator, giving CPR, and when I entered they all looked at me with such sorrow in their faces. I said my goodbyes and then they wheeled me back to recovery.

Exactly 30 minutes later, a doctor from Children's Memorial called and said, "I am so sorry, but your daughter has an undeveloped windpipe, and her esophagus is in her stomach. There is nothing we can do, we are transporting back so you can be with her when she passes". I quickly asked "Can you donate her organs? The Dr. said, "That is very kind of you, but I am not sure, we will see."

By the time they returned, I was in a room and they brought her in. They stopped doing CPR, and they put her in my arms, it was like cradling a little football. Her eyes never opened, all my family was around. She made no sound except when she took her final breath.

The hardest part for me:
Leaving the hospital when they wheeled me downstairs and all the other mothers had balloons on their wheelchairs and their babies in their laps.

Helpful things from family and friends:
I received a few nice letters, daily phone calls from my dad. Finding, SHARING, and reading others people's stories.

Things that have helped me cope and deal with the heartache:
I realized, I was fortunate enough to even get pregnant and feel the baby inside me as some never have this chance.

I have learned:
No pregnancy is safe until delivery. A lot can happen, and no one talks about it, until something awful happens.

How I keep my baby's memory alive:

- For the first year, I would remember her on the 19th of every month.
- Balloon launches on her b-day.
- The chance to tell people when they ask if I have any other children. I say yes, my 1st born died.
- Donated $10,000 to SHARE so they could become more visible, so more people would know about their mission.
- Every time I hear that a child's name is "Eden", my heart gets warm.
- Every time I see the number 3:33 on a building, at the gas station, on the clock, I feel that is a "sign" from her.

Additional words:
Obviously I was devastated when she passed, but I felt fortunate enough that I had the experience of being pregnant, experiencing delivery, and that she did not suffer. It was beyond tragic and I had a drawing of her made which I have in my office.

~ Linda Gidwitz Karamitis ~

They say there is a reason,
They say that time will heal,
But neither time nor reason,
Will change the way I feel,
For no-one knows the heartache,
That lies behind our smiles,
No-one knows how many times,
We have broken down and cried,
We want to tell you something,
So there won't be any doubt,
You're so wonderful to think of,
But so hard to be without.

~ Unknown

CHAPTER 11

Collin Joseph MacGregor

November 15, 2009 – January 8, 2010

My story:
In October 2009, when I was 21 weeks pregnant with our 2nd child (our oldest was almost 2 at the time), we went for a long weekend away to Florida to visit my husband's parents (we live in Ohio). On October 17, I woke up in the middle of the night at my in-laws' house with an awful pain in my right side. I was crying and yelling for my husband, Mike, to wake up. We went to a nearby hospital and learned my appendix had burst. They removed my appendix, and we were all so relieved that our baby was still okay! They released me from the hospital, but a few hours later, I went into labor and back to the hospital. After almost 3 weeks in FL hospitals, they allowed me to fly home to OH if I went directly

to the hospital so I could be on bed-rest there, with my doctors and in our hometown.

The next couple of weeks were difficult, as I kept going into labor and they'd try to stop it. I finally went into unstoppable labor when I was 25 weeks 6 days pregnant and they did an emergency C-section. Collin was born on November 15, weighing 1 pound 15 ounces and was 12.99 inches long.

The first month of Collin's life was great, despite the overwhelming nature of having a baby in the NICU. He was strong, developing, and healthy. He then developed some issues and some things happened in the hospital and we were transferred to the Cleveland Clinic, where they treat the most critical babies. Collin's health began to improve, as the doctors and nurses did everything they could for him, but his final surgery just didn't work as it should have, and Collin died in my arms surrounded by his family.

The hardest part for me:
I just miss him. My heart aches for that little boy and nothing can seem to fill that void. I also hate talking to new people and trying to explain how many children I have.

Helpful things from family and friends:
My mother-in-law sent a text message on the 8th and 15th of every month for the first year, telling us she was thinking about us and Collin. She still sends a message on his birthday and on the anniversary of the day he died.

A friend called me all of the time and left voice mails. I hardly ever called back, but she still called anyway. My sister-in-law had a quilt made out of square pieces of Collin's clothes. A co-worker often would leave a Starbucks gift card (my favorite coffee) on my desk.

Things that have helped me cope and deal with the heartache:
Writing helps...I had a care-page for Collin for his last couple weeks of life, and I continue to post updates occasionally. Unfortunately, a good friend of mine has a son who died when he was four months old, just 10 months after Collin died. While it is heart-wrenching to have a friend go through this deep sadness, it does help to have someone who understands. Oh, and a good cup of strong black coffee never hurt either. :-)

I have learned:
I have learned that I am not sure it really gets easier, although I am a little better at hiding my sadness. I have learned that although people do have good intentions, sometimes they say really ridiculous things, although I can't blame them, as I don't even know what to say...it is just really an awful situation!

How I keep my baby's memory alive:
My husband and I, along with our friends who lost their son, have started Kisses from Heaven, which we hope will attain non-profit status in the next couple of months. What we do is put together gift bags of items NICU

parents need during their stay with their baby. We currently deliver the bags to 5 area hospitals in December, as that is the time we were in the NICU, but we are looking to expand and deliver packages at a couple of other times throughout the year.

We also do acts of kindness for strangers, we release balloons and have cupcakes on Collin's birthday, and Collin has a small Christmas tree that we hang all of his ornaments on. We buy a new ornament each year to add to the tree.

~ Jill MacGregor ~

And God shall wipe away all tears from their eyes; and there shall be no more death, neither sorrow, nor crying, neither shall there be any more pain: for the former things are passed away.

Revelation 21:4

Gabriella Rose Shen

July 3, 2013

My Story:
My name is Marybel Shen. My husband, Matt, and I have been married a year and in March 2013, we found out we were expecting! We were overjoyed. We had suffered an early miscarriage in December 2012 so this would be our rainbow baby! Words could not describe our excitement. We went in to our 8 week visit and got to meet our little nugget. She was beautiful - I could just tell. At our 12 week visit, my doctor explained we would only do a Doppler to find the heartbeat. I remember him putting the gel onto the transducer and as he did he explained that it usually takes a few minutes to find the baby's heartbeat. As he said it and placed it on my abdomen, my angel's beautiful, and STRONG, heartbeat could be heard! She was very

cooperative! Matt and I decided to go to an outside facility for a gender ultrasound on June 15, 2013 at 17 weeks. That's when we found out we were having a girl! Matt cried with joy and I couldn't stop smiling. I was going to have a little princess! I could get all those cute little dresses and bows I had longingly admired at stores. I couldn't wait until November - her due date was November 23, 2013. The following two weeks passed with no problems. Gabby had become more and more active and she loved to do flips and kick like crazy! I loved feeling her little feet dancing within me. That has been the most amazing feeling I've ever experienced. On Wednesday July, 30, 2013 at 5:30 am, I woke up to go to the bathroom - and I was bleeding. My heart stopped and fear came over me. I woke Matt up and we decided to go to the Emergency Room. Upon arrival, they did an exam and an ultrasound. Gabby was doing well, except, I was dilated to 3 cm and her tiny foot was passing through my cervix. They wheeled me to labor and delivery. The rest is a haze. Several doctors came to see me and talked to me. We decided to let nature run its course and see if labor would cease or progress. It progressed. Before long, I was in full blown labor and at 7:20 pm, Gabriella Rose was born. She was beautiful. My nurse, Jackie, dressed her in a lovely pink dress and hat, made just for her. I remember her tiny feet and hands - so precious. She looked just like her daddy. We got to spend the night with our angel and the next day I was discharged. It was the most heart wrenching feeling to have to leave the hospital and my baby would not. We had arranged for the funeral home to pick her up later that day. I was totally lost the next few days. The funeral was held on Monday July 8 at Assumption Cemetery. My heart shattered into a million pieces as I watched as Gabby was buried. To this day I feel an emptiness in my heart where Gabby should be.

The hardest part for me has been trying to cope with the fact that I will never be able to hold my little girl. Seeing pregnant women and knowing they will soon have their own baby makes me miss Gabby more and more. Seeing all the pretty dresses that I once hoped I would buy for Gabby and knowing she'll never wear them.

Helpful things from family and friends have been their insistence on bringing me back out into the world. If it were up to me, I'd spend my days at home in bed and sitting by Gabby's grave. But my family has helped me understand that Gabs would not want this for me and that there are other ways to keep her memory alive.

Things that have helped me cope and deal with the heartache has been talking about Gabby. I only held her in my womb for 20 short weeks but I have so many memories of those weeks. I remember that she disliked Chinese food greatly! I thought this was a bit funny - and ironic - because her daddy is Chinese. He, however, did not find it as funny! Hahaha! Her favorite food was pepperoni pizza, so every 3rd of the month Matt and I celebrate Gabby by eating pepperoni pizza for dinner. I just love those memories of my sweet angel.

I have learned:
In the past short months I have learned that the fact that my baby is in heaven does not mean that I am not a mother. Some days are more difficult and I have to try harder to remind myself of this. I feel like a mother. I had to give my baby back and that will always be the hardest thing I've done in my life, but I still have a baby and I am a mother.

How I keep my baby's memory alive:
I keep Gabby's memory alive by remembering to have pepperoni pizza on the 3rd of each month (no complaints with this one!), we have a balloon release each month to celebrate my angel and I talk about her daily.

Every day is different with my feelings. Some days I'm sad. Others I'm angry. But every single day...I miss my Gabby Rose.

~ Marybel Shen ~

Rest Gently With Me

Startled and fascinated by the beauty and fragility
of your wings, I watch as you move
so gently
so quietly
almost unexpectedly
through my world.

And then I watch as you move on,
fluttering softly into the distance.
Pleading silently, I beg you,
please ... don't go.

I haven't yet had the time
to memorize
to remember
to understand
the uniqueness of the beauty that is yours.

I know I cannot hold you for long,
capturing you for my world.
But, rest gently with me
if only for a moment.

That I may treasure the memory
and the beauty of the
gift that you are.

~ Unknown

CHAPTER 13

Ceiliedh Madison Burger

July 2, 2010

My Story:
Taking myself back to the first day I became a mom, is not a happy one. It is bittersweet. I wish I could say different, but then I would be denying my daughter. I would be denying who she was and who she is, and who she will be to me forever. July 2, 2010 at 8:30 pm, I held my daughter who had already passed away. She came into existence February 18th by way of a bright blue plus sign on a pregnancy test. We were so excited to become new parents. Her first ultrasound was April 11, 2010. She was perfect, my little peanut. Strong heartbeat, perfect body; a dream was born.

Her second ultrasound was June 28th. We found out we had a girl, but something was not right. The technology in Glenwood Springs is limited, as we are very rural. They referred us to Skyridge Medical in Lonetree, Colorado. We scheduled an appointment for June 30th. Those were the two longest days of my life. I had no idea what was about to happen, no clue how crushed my heart would be, or the depth to which my soul would be ripped.

June 30th. My mother and I drove to Lonetree and I still remember the stale smell of the facility and the climb to the waiting room, opening the heavy door, the paperwork for insurance as it sat on my belly, my baby. The rising anxiety and fear had swelled from the pit of my stomach to the back of my throat. My breathing was shaky, heavy, laden with anticipation and the unknown.

The rest was a blur. The voice of the Doctor rings through my spirit still today as a cold wind, "Amanda, Nancy. This baby has fatal birth defects and will not live."

Remember the twin towers? I fell harder, faster, into blackness, into despair, into the abyss. My baby girl, yes a daughter, would die.

She had a healthy strong loud heartbeat that paid testament to her personal strength as she became a rare baby who did not pass away when her amniotic sac had torn 4-8 weeks into gestation. She fought the odds and won. Unfortunately the bands that remained when the sac resealed, forever altered her growth, and took her life in the bondage of attaching themselves to her, to prevent further healthy development. Everything below the sternum had developed on the outside. She had no big healthy baby tummy. Her spine was curved at a 90 degree, her feet clubbed. Her life was dependent on the amniotic fluid, not air. She would not survive delivery.

I found myself in the bathroom at some point in all that. My hair was a rat's nest, my face splotched red. In that face, I saw a broken soul. A hollow face, swollen with grief, stricken by shock, and devastated by loss of control. A mother, but a mother without a child to hold, too soon.

The medical staff encouraged me to stay in Denver and start the process of inducing labor and delivering. I couldn't do it. I had to go home. I had to hug my husband, cry, breathe. Anything. Anything but say goodbye.

My mother drove me part of the way home, the rest of way I drove. I somehow made it to my front door unscathed. The wet eyes of my husband greeted me. With a hug. We named her Ceiliedh Madison that night. And decided to go back the next day and deliver her. We wanted her to feel no pain, to bear no grievances, so we had made the hardest decision we have ever, or will ever make. That Thursday morning I cried. That day, I cried

We drove to Presbyterian St. Luke's that evening and delivered our sweet girl after 21 hours of drugs, silence, awkward moments, and two epidurals. At 8:30 pm I delivered my stillborn daughter. I held her small body in my arms. I had waterfalls flowing down my cheeks, drenching her baby blanket.

"I had so many dreams for you, so many hopes." That is what I remember telling her. I know I told I was so sorry I couldn't save her, and that she had other things she needed to do. I kissed her, touched her, held her. I didn't hold her long enough, or kiss her enough, or hug her enough. I will never get over that. I said good-bye. I hold that forever in my heart, those moments.

We went home, I printed up and mailed out birth-death announcements:

Ceiliedh Madison Burger
Delivered into this world
And back into the arms of Mother Nature
At 8:30 pm on July 2, 2010
Grant us the
Serenity to accept things we cannot change,
Courage to change the things we can, and the
Wisdom to know the difference
Patience for the things that take time
Appreciation for all that we have, and
Tolerance for those with different struggles
Freedom to live beyond the limitations of our past ways, the
Ability to feel your love for us and our love for each other and the
Strength to get up and try again even when we feel it is hopeless.

The hardest part for me:
I left Presbytarin St. Luke with a broken spirit and was a skeleton of a woman. All that I was had died. I entered back into society a lost mother, a bereaved mother.

America holds no space, no patience, no understanding for a woman who's baby had died. It was hardest for me to find myself again, to find a sense of my new normal, my new life, and still hold onto the memories without holding onto the anger, the sense of bereft emptiness and to accept that everything had changed. I am still healing, still struggling, but my anchors in this world are my two rainbow babies, Skyelar and Zebulon. Without them, my heart would ache, wanting to hold Ceiliedh again.

I have learned to love again, to live again, to laugh and breathe once more. But there is always a sliver of the bittersweet joyous sorrow that caresses my thoughts, my laugh, my tears, my hugs, my words, my vision.

Helpful things from family and friends:

Time and hugs. Cards serve as such a wonderful tangible gift that I can go back and read, and remind myself how much she was loved, how much I am loved. Flowers die; words either fall on deaf ears or a shattered heart and that space is so tender, words can often perforate or sear the already hurting heart when the speaker does not intend to harm, but to heal. Silence in hugs is the best of you don't know what to say. Just hold them, because we are barely standing, barely breathing. Because the pain is so severe, even breathing feels like drowning.

Do not hide, throw away, or remove baby items. A bereaved mother has already lost a lifetime of loving her baby, watching them grow, taking pictures, and taking them all in. She has lost control, lost a sense of faith, and has lost herself. Those baby items are all that is left and some of us, it is too painful to keep them, but we will ask you to take them away, or we will ask you to help us enshrine them in some way to keep what we have left, in a safe place so we can return to them time to time. I slept with her baby blanket for a long time. It is now folded under the small blue velvet bag in which her ashes came back to me. I don't have much, which is a huge regret. I have her hat, blanket, foot prints, her bag that held her ashes, and only my memories of holding her, and one good picture. One.

Things that have helped me cope and deal with the heartache:
My memories, her picture and her belongings, and those friends and family that just simply hold a space for me and allow me the time, the relapse; the shifting of my tides of grief, because it never goes away. It haunts me every day, but each day, I know I am getting stronger. I deal with the heartache every day because it wounded me so badly. I can never fully recover, as I was forever changed. But with those things, and the incredible support, I came to learn how to feel again. And to feel love, joy, hope. Not just anger and sadness.

I also spread her ashes in the ocean on her due date that following November. It helped with closure, with grappling with the circumstances, and accepting what had happened. I chose water because it carries a cycle of life that is eternal and it travels everywhere so I know whenever the rain falls, or the ice freezes, she is: dust to dust: all around me.

How I keep my baby's memory alive:
That August after Ceiliedh passed away, I was driving along the same road that took me to Denver. I saw hundreds of Black Eyed Susan's line the highway, swaying gently in the warm autumn breeze. I distinctly heart her voice say to me "Hello Mommy! I'm okay!" Since that moment, these have always been her flower. Two weeks later, while rafting down the river, we pulled out and took a break. A dragonfly came and sat on my husband knee, and then flew to me and landed on my shoulder and just sat there. Everyone travelling with us knew it was her, saying hello.

Whenever I see a sunflower or a dragonfly, I think of my sweet Ceiliedh. I honor her on her birthday, on her due date, and I celebrate Christmas now with a Blue Christmas that our church offers. It is a Christmas for those who suffer a loss and that the holidays hold a different meaning for us. I honor her by holding others who have to suffer the same tragedy.

Additional Words:
She is alive, in my heart always, teaching me, guiding me, and loving me. She sings in the voices of the birds outside my window, she kisses my cheek in every ray of sunshine, she dances in every rainbow that graces my eyes, and she flies on the wings of every bird, butterfly, and creature with wings. She is everywhere, but my arms.

No parent should ever have to bury their child and live with the heartache, but we somehow do. And many of us do it with valor, honor, and without reserve or fear that our emotions will be judged because we have walked a road that often takes the heart of the happiest person and would turn it dark if it were not for the saving grace of faith, courage, and hope.

I write this to honor her memory, to tell her story so that not only other bereaved parents know they are not alone, and to pass her legacy onto her siblings who are my rainbow babies, born in the calm of the storm: Skyelar Brie and Zebulon Hawkins.

In memory of Ceiliedh Madison Burger, delivered into this world and back into the arms of Mother Nature at 8:30 pm, July 2, 2010.

*~ **Amanda Leah Emerson-Burger** ~*

Trust in the Lord with all thine heart; and lean not unto thine own understanding.

Proverbs 3:5

Kaia and Ezra

October 7, 2008

My story:
I found out I was pregnant August 2008. October 7, 2008, I woke up to go use the bathroom and out came a big round ball of blood about the size of a silver dollar coin. I woke up my boyfriend and we rushed to the E.R., we were there for 12 hours. They ran tests, got blood from me, gave me a shot, and gave me a big pad because I was bleeding a lot by this time already. They gave me an ultrasound and then the OBGYN at the E.R. told us that we were pregnant with twins and that I'm miscarrying them. It sounded like I just lost a pair of keys the way she had said it. I said, "Excuse me, did you just say twins?!" She replied, "Yes and one twin died a week before this." My jaw dropped! I didn't know it was twins! We also found out it was a boy and girl. Twins didn't run in our

families. We already had names picked out for a boy and for a girl so we just used both for the twins. The lady at the E.R didn't even tell me what I was going to go through or what the process was for miscarrying. It was my first pregnancy. We go home as if everything is okay. A couple hours later, I was walking to the bathroom and I felt wetness come down my leg. I didn't think I had peed myself so I wasn't sure what it was. I used the bathroom and then they dropped out of me. I looked and they're they were, helpless; it left me in the bathroom crying and screaming. We scooped them out of the toilet and went to my OBGYN the next day and gave them the twins. I went into depression after that for a long time. I would cry and rock myself to sleep inside of our closet. I wouldn't leave the house or do anything. I felt like a robot doing the same things every day, but never getting to talk about my feelings. I grieved terribly for a couple of years. My doctor wanted to put me on depression pills, but I told him no and that I would try other things before taking pills. I started going back to church and that helped a great deal. Before I knew it, my depression went away and I was able to talk about the miscarriage. I always push for people to talk about their miscarriage because not a lot of people do. People think it's a taboo subject, but it's not and it shouldn't be.

The hardest part for me:
Accepting the fact that the children I was looking forward to having in my life would no longer be born to me in April 2009. I couldn't understand how I loved my

children so much already and didn't even meet them. Also, hearing them come out of me in the toilet and then seeing them was the most devastating thing for me ever in my life because I felt so helpless.

Helpful things from family and friends:
I had my friends with me who helped me. They would come over and help with things or they would just comfort me and hug me and let me know that everything would be okay.

Things that have helped me cope and deal with the heartache:
I would do things in memory of them and that helped. The things that I had bought for them, I gave to close friends who were having babies. Going to church also helped me cope and deal with the heartache. I journaled a lot and did things for me that I enjoyed doing that would get my mind off of it so I wouldn't grieve so hard.

I have learned:
That everything will be okay, it takes time and doesn't go right away, people grieve differently, and that it's okay to grieve even if it is for a long time. Also, that God gives and God takes away but blessed be the name of The Lord. Third, surround yourself with people who are supportive and loving.

How I keep my baby's memory alive:
I'll do paintings in memory of them or I go to balloon releases.

Additional words:
Women are not alone. They should be able to talk to other people about this and not keep it hidden. It's not good to keep this in. Surround yourself with good, loving and supportive people who like to give and receive hugs (only if you're a hugger like me) ;).

~ Alyssa Takeshita ~

To some you are forgotten,
To others, just the past,
But to us who loved and lost you,
Your memory will always last.

I'll always be there with you,
And watch the sky at night.
Find the brightest star that's gleaming
That's my halo shining bright.

You'll see me in the morning frost
That mists your windowpane.
That's me, in the summer showers,
I'll be dancing in the rain.

When you feel a gentle breeze
From a gentle wind that blows,
That's me! I'll be there,
Planting a kiss upon your nose.

When you see a child playing
And your heart feels a little tug
That's me! I'll be there,
Giving your heart a hug.

So Daddy, please don't look so sad.
Mummy don't you cry.
I'm in the arms of friends,
And they sing me lullabies.

~Unknown

CHAPTER 15

Benjamin Spencer Klimaszewski

January 7, 1998   January 12, 1998

My story:
After 4 years of marriage my husband and I decided to have a baby and the next month I was pregnant! Being that I would be 35 when I was going to deliver I had a level 2 ultrasound and an amnio which both showed that we were expecting a healthy baby boy - who was due on January 31,1998.

On January 6 - I went into labor early - and on January 7th – our beautiful baby boy Benjamin was born. The Doctor told us although he was a little early - he was fine and that we would both be discharged on January 10th. The morning of January 10 the pediatrician came in to discharge him and I had mentioned to the Dr that our boy had not had a bowel movement - yet. Being a first time mom - I did not know that was a huge issue. The Dr said - well we can DC you - but the baby will need to stay - BUT - don't be concerned - it is something that an enema will fix in no time. We stayed in the family room on the L&D floor and at 1:00 am - the Dr. woke us to say our baby was showing signs of distress - his abdomen was beginning to swell and he was spitting up and not taking any formula/breast milk. The Dr had the nerve to tell us that even though our baby was in distress - he did not think it was worth bothering his colleague at another hospital with a NICU at that time of morning... I trusted the Dr - so did not argue. By the time our baby was transferred it was late afternoon that next day.

When he got to the hospital with the NICU - they also told us not to be overly concerned - that it was nothing life threatening and they would do a barium enema on him. After that he just went from bad to worse. His abdomen was beginning to get more and more distended. He was rushed into emergency surgery and they performed an illeostomy on him - he didn't do well at all after the surgery – we were never allowed to hold him again when he was alive - as he was so sick. On the morning of Jan. 12 - he was rushed into surgery again - as his illeostomy was not working and the stoma was turning black. Once they got him into surgery - they found he did not have enough good bowel to survive - we had no choice but to take him off of life support. It was the saddest day of our lives. We went from having what we thought was a perfectly healthy baby to making funeral arrangements in a matter of 5 days. We were devastated.

The funeral was a blur - the sadness and depression was unbearable.

The hardest part for me:
The hardest part for me was the emptiness that I felt and sometimes the lack of compassion from others. Going to the mall was pure torture - babies and strollers - pregnant women everywhere. Even being around our young nieces and nephews was so painful.

Helpful things from family and friends:
Family and friends would be most helpful when they would listen to us talk about Benjamin. What we didn't want to hear was well at least he was just 5 days old and you weren't too attached to him or - don't worry - you will have another baby soon. We wanted Benjamin - he was planned for.

We found a support group that specialized in infant loss - that was very helpful to be around others who knew and shared our grief. We had a wonderful social worker who facilitated the group - she would listen to our story and our sadness month after month - for years after years.

We took one day at a time. Sometimes it was one step forward - 2 steps back. The firsts were so hard - birthdays, holidays. Mothers Day and Father's Day were the worst. Sometimes the anticipation was worse than the actual day itself.

Things that have helped me cope and deal with the heartache:
The only thing that helped me cope and made the days bearable was the thought of having another baby. It took us 4 years - but in 2002 we finally brought home a beautiful baby boy who we adopted from S. Korea. He made life complete for us again and I felt whole for the first time in years.

How I keep my baby's memory alive:
Every year we attend a memorial service at the hospital where Benjamin was born - it is specialized for those who have suffered the loss of an infant. The service is held in December and each set of parents get a special ornament to bring home to put on their Christmas tree - we now have 16 of these ornaments....We also take part in 2 national candlelight services in honor of Benjamin and we encourage our close family to do the same.

Additional words:
There is no greater loss in this world - than the loss of a baby – but it is survivable - even though some days you will think it isn't. I know that we will see our Benjamin again in the next life - but until then - we will continue to think about and miss him every single day.

Thank you for this opportunity to let the world know: Benjamin Spencer Klimaszewski did exist and will live on in our hearts forever.

~ Robin Klimaszewski ~

*I sought the LORD, and he heard me,
and delivered me from all my fears.
The righteous cry, and the LORD heareth,
and delivereth them out of all their troubles.*

Psalms 34:4,17

CHAPTER 16

Lucas Edward Eshleman

May 17, 2001 – May 20, 2011

My Story:
My pregnancy was completely normal. I took my prenatal vitamins every day, got plenty of rest and exercise, and overall felt great. I only had one ultrasound during my pregnancy. I had scheduled the appointment four weeks earlier and I crossed each day off my calendar as it got closer. I loved my baby from the moment I saw the red line slowly appear on the pregnancy test. My love grew stronger with each passing day and I couldn't wait to see him or her on the monitor. I remember lying on the table filled with anticipation and excitement, while trying to ignore my full, uncomfortable bladder.

The cold gel was squeezed onto my belly and the first image we saw was confirmation that we were having a boy. There was no question, and my husband and I were filled with happiness and delight. We knew his name was going to be Lucas. He was moving, kicking and full of life. The joy I felt was immense. The sonographer measured his head, legs, heart, etc. We were told everything looked fine and I was given one small photo profiling Lucas' face. He was precious and beautiful.

We scheduled a C-section because both of my previous pregnancies had resulted in cesarean sections after 12 to 24 hours of labor. My due date fell on May 24th which ironically is my mother's birthday. My surgery was scheduled one week prior to my due date which fell on May 17th.

When that day finally came I was anxious and excited, but scared and nervous as well. I couldn't wait to hold Lucas in my arms, to gaze into his eyes and to whisper words of love to him.

My first spinal anesthesia injection did not work. I could feel the cold, wet cotton ball as they rubbed it on my stomach. I had been through this before and I knew that I should be able to feel the sensation of it, but not the cold wetness of it. "It's still cold." I told my doctor over and over again, to ensure that he didn't start the incision before he should. After several minutes, and several more cotton ball tests, they decided it must have been a "bad batch." I had to sit up, hang my legs over the side of the table, and bend over my knees again to receive another spinal injection. This time the cold cotton ball did not feel cold and the surgery began.

As I said, I had been through this before and I knew it wouldn't be long now. I would see my son's gorgeous face within the next few minutes. I felt a little pull and my doctor could see the head. He told me he had a lot of hair and my exhilaration grew. I squeezed my husband's hand, and out of excitement I encouraged him to peek behind the curtain so that he could see Lucas being born. Within seconds the room fell silent. There were two doctors, two nurses, an anesthesiologist and a pediatric team. Minutes before, I could hear them talking amongst themselves and getting ready to assist; now I could have heard a pin drop. After my husband snuck a peek, he became faint and had to be escorted out of the operating room. I had no idea what was going on, but naturally I knew something wasn't right. I kept asking my doctor if everything was okay. He didn't answer me but requested additional medical personnel. I laid there helpless and scared. I couldn't move. My mind was racing and the minutes seemed like hours. What was happening?!

Finally my doctor acknowledged the question I had been repeatedly asking. "You're baby appears to have some deformities and we are trying to figure it out." I said nothing. I couldn't see, but I sensed that they were frantically in the process of cleaning Lucas. I could hear him crying; his beautiful, individual sound. Little did I know, I wouldn't hear his cry again.

As the doctors were finishing up my surgery, they brought Lucas over beside my head so that I could admire him. He was beautiful with brown hair and dark brown eyes. I tried to soothe him with my voice. I told him that I loved him as they rushed him out of the room. I was told he was turning gray and that they needed to get him to the NICU.

I lay there frightened as I was tugged and pulled at, and put back together again. The emotions I felt were overwhelming. I was dazed and confused. The hospital staff was counting supplies and tools, but the room was no longer upbeat and optimistic as it had been in the beginning. How could my emotions change so drastically, so quickly?

They took me to the recovery room, only this time I didn't have a baby waiting for me as I did with my previous pregnancies. My mom came in, her eyes full of worry and concern. I felt sad for her as this should have been a happy moment in her life. What was happening? I wanted my baby and I wanted him now! Although I was worried, I was sure he would be fine. I knew the NICU would give Lucas what he needed and he would come home with us. I was so wrong.

I lost all track of time but once I was able to wiggle my toes, I was helped into a wheelchair and wheeled down the hall to see Lucas. The nurses took a few Polaroid photos. Looking back at those photos, I had a big smile on my face. I was ecstatic to see Lucas and to be able to hold his hand. His fingers and little toes were webbed and I clearly didn't comprehend how serious Lucas' condition was. He was hooked up to several machines with tubes taped to him from head to toe. Lucas squeezed my finger and there we sat for the next hour or so. It was extremely difficult to go back to my hospital room without him. This is not how it was supposed to go.

Lucas was born at 10:56 a.m. It was now midnight and the doctors still didn't have any answers. Finally at 2 a.m. the next morning, a doctor I had never met before came in and sat down at the end of my bed. He had white hair and kind, soft eyes. Lucas was born with Aperts Syndrome he told us, and a serious heart defect. He was in the process of being transferred to a bigger hospital about 40 miles south. I was exhausted, but couldn't sleep. My son was alone in an ambulance, experiencing sounds and sensations that were foreign to him. My heart was breaking. *Was he wondering where I was? Was he cold? Hungry? Scared? And was he missing me as much as I was missing him?* Oh how I wanted to rewind time and be back home; in my warm bed, feeling Lucas' carefree kicking and movement, where I could talk to him and tell him everything was going to be alright.

I was scheduled to stay in the hospital I was at for three nights, but they discharged me the very next day so that I could take the 55-minute drive to see Lucas. The hospital he was at didn't have a room available for me so my husband and I stayed at a Ronald McDonald House nearby. The second day there I woke up in extreme pain. My body was ready to feed Lucas and my breasts were as hard as rocks, but there was no relief. Lucas had to be fed through tubes because he was born with a cleft palette. The roof of his mouth didn't develop normally (which left an opening in the palate that goes through to the nasal cavity). Some of the tubes attached to him interfered with his voice box; therefore, we couldn't hear his voice. The heat lamps seemed to bother his sensitive, baby skin and he was uncomfortable at times. We would see him crying but there was no sound. We could see his silent cry, and it was heart wrenching.

We gowned up, washed our hands and arms all the way up to our elbows and visited him as often as we could.

We met with a team of doctors and it didn't look good. They drew pictures of Lucas' underdeveloped heart trying to describe the defect. They tried to explain what they would have to do to repair it. It would take three surgeries. The heart surgeons could try to do this, this, and this – their words and medical terminology were escaping my brain before they could register. I nodded in unison with my husband as I tried to focus. Why is this not making any sense? *Think, think, think!* My mind was screaming.

After the heart surgeons explained their specialty and put their sketches of Lucas's heart away, another team of surgeons explained that Lucas would require about eight surgeries due to him being born with Apert's Syndrome. And unfortunately these eight surgeries would have a better success rate if Lucas was born with a normal and strong heart.

"It looks grim." Someone in the room said.

"So where would we start?" My husband asked trying to remain level headed.

What did they expect us to say? We just wanted them to fix our precious baby boy. The baby boy we thought would be born perfectly healthy. Now they were talking about eleven major surgeries, but it didn't seem as if they were talking about these surgeries happening to the same baby. It kind of seemed as if the two teams were talking about two different patients; one with a heart defect and one with Apert's Syndrome.

"We don't know what you should do." One of the heart surgeons said. "But the heart surgeries would need to take place first, and I have to tell you that there is no guarantee he would survive the first surgery. I'm sorry but I need to make that clear. It's a considerably low percentage of babies who survive the first surgery."

"There is a lot to consider here." The doctor continued. "As you know, Lucas is on life support, and as tough a subject as this is, you also have to consider whether or not you want to keep him on it. Another option for you to consider is whether you want to forgo the surgeries and take him off life support."

I cleared my throat. "So what would YOU do if you were in our situation?" I asked, desperately hoping for a clear answer.

"That's a tough one, and I'm sorry I don't know." The doctor replied, looking around the room at the other doctors. None of them had an answer. "Why don't you go back to your room at the Ronald McDonald house and think about it tonight. You can let us know what you decide in the morning."

Just as we were getting ready to leave the room and thank the doctors for their time, a nurse came in with some new information. One of the doctors motioned for us to hold on for a minute, so we sat back down in our seats and waited.

"Okay" the doctor took a deep breath before continuing, "These reports show that Lucas seems to have a lot of fluid on his lungs so unfortunately we would not be able to perform any surgeries on him at this time. We also found that he doesn't appear to have a Corpus Callosum. The Corpus Callosum connects the left and right cerebral hemispheres of the brain to provide communication between the two sides. This is a birth defect and the effects can be mild to severe depending on the level of brain abnormality. This is definitely something else for you to consider."

My husband and I left the room feeling defeated. Can't they just fix him so we can take him home? I kept wondering.

We wanted to see Lucas before we left for the night so we scrubbed and gowned up before entering the NICU. He was on the very end of a long row of crib-like beds, and we could see him as we walked down what seemed to be a very long isle. I could see him laying there in just his diaper under a heat lamp. He was crying but no sound was being produced. He was silently crying... again. His belly looked red and sore and irritated; from the heat lamp I presumed. We talked to him and tried to comfort him before we left. He looked very uncomfortable with all of the tubes attached to him - held on by big strips of tape; to his face, and head, and feet. His sweet cheeks were scrunched together beneath the clear tape. I felt the urge to readjust it but didn't dare, worried that I might cause more discomfort. I couldn't help but wonder what he was thinking as we left. Did he wonder why we were leaving him or when we'd be back? Was he lonely laying there all by his lonesome?

We had to go to the grocery store before we went back to our room at the Ronald McDonald house. They had a kitchen we could use, but we needed to get a few things for ourselves. We walked around in a daze as everyone went about their seemingly happy business. How could no one know what we were going through? Did they not realize that we just had to leave our newborn baby and that we had a huge decision to make? A decision that we didn't want to make! Did the friendly cashier think we were being rude because we weren't responding to her cheerful "Hi! How are you today?" greeting?

My husband held my hand as we walked out of the grocery store. There was a chill in the air and my body ached everywhere.

"So many complications." I said as I slowly lowered myself into the car. "I can't help but feel as though Lucas is trying to make this decision a bit easier on us. They couldn't even operate right now if they wanted to because of the fluid on his lungs. And he'd require eleven surgeries to get to where? And what exactly does it mean that he was born without a Corpus Callo thingy?"

"It seems like every time we turn around there is a new complication they are telling us about. I don't know what we should do." My husband replied as he lowered his head into his hands.

"Me either. I wish we had a computer so that we could do some research. It hurts to see Lucas in pain under the heat lamp. I can't tell what he needs or wants. And if they could do the surgery the doctor said he may not even survive the first one. I'd hate to think of him dying on the operating table. And what's causing the fluid on his lungs? None of this makes sense to me. I just want to go home with our little boy. His crib, and bassinette, and bouncy chair are waiting at home." I sighed. "And what does taking him off life support even mean really?" I asked my husband.

"We'll ask in the morning." He solemnly replied.

We didn't sleep that night. We talked, tossed and turned, and cried. My incision was really red and sore, my head pounded, my body hurt; but my heart hurt more.

The next morning we went back to the hospital. Lucas's condition hadn't changed. He looked very uncomfortable with the evidence of needle pokes everywhere; on his head, on his arms, on his feet; and he was silently crying.

The nurses pulled up a rocking chair and asked if I wanted to hold him. They helped each other carefully pick him and all of his connecting tubes up, and slowly lowered him onto my lap. I was scared to make the slightest movement out of fear of accidently touching or bumping one of the tubes. He had new pieces of tape stuck to the far sides of his cheeks holding the tubes in place, and sticky residue from the old tape that needed to be washed off. I told him how much I loved him and gently kissed his forehead. I yearned to breast feed him and my body's natural instincts kicked in as well, causing more pain. Lucas couldn't even eat if he wanted to because of how his mouth formed, or hadn't formed. I tried rocking him gently, but he was still silently crying and it seemed like nothing was consoling him. We tried to put his pacifier in, in hopes of calming him down. He appeared even more uncomfortable in my lap and I felt helpless. His silent cries were becoming more and more intense and I asked the nurses to help me put him back in his crib like hospital bed. Once there he slowly calmed down, but he still didn't look anywhere near content.

"Okay, so he can't have surgery due to his condition. So, what… what would happen if we want to discuss taking him off life support?" I asked one of the head nurses.

She explained that they would unhook him from everything and basically rush him into a private room with us where we could say goodbye. She said we may only have a few minutes.

My heart sank. Say goodbye? Although it made sense, it definitely didn't make sense… if that makes sense. It was sinking in. I had a flashback to a few days earlier in the operating room when Lucas was born. The doctor said "We have to get him out of here and to the NICU. He's turning gray." Yes, being taken off life support meant exactly how it sounded.

My husband and I looked at each other, and then we looked at Lucas attached to all the tubes and breathing ventilators and it was as if we knew what the right decision was, but we didn't want to say it out loud.

We made the decision to take him off the life support. We waited at the end of the NICU, near the door, while they unhooked him. One of the nurses took Lucas in her arms and walked as fast as she could towards us directing us out of the NICU and into a private room. Some of our family was waiting there.

We held him skin to skin. We kissed him all over. There were no longer tubes restricting our love from him. For the first time Lucas looked content and calm. He looked peaceful and immediately stopped crying.

Lucas died on May 20th. During his short time on Earth he showed his love in amazing ways. He was pronounced dead at 6:08 pm as I was holding him, and I was crying hysterically. All of the sudden he slowly opened his eyes and looked up at me. My hysteria eased as I looked into his dark eyes. "If he's gone, why is he looking at me?" I asked the doctor who checked his pulse again and was openly surprised. Lucas was alive. I imagined him speaking to God, telling him that his mommy wasn't ready yet and to please give him just a little more time.

For the next two hours, my husband and I cradled him between us, and whispered our goodbyes. We promised that we'd take care of each other. We told him we'd be okay and that he could go. And a few moments later he did. His Spirit left his body, and we undeniably felt the difference when it did. There was no question that he was no longer there in our arms. It was only his earthly shell. He was gone.

The nurse came and gently took him from us. I fell into my husband's chest and let out a wailing cry like never before. This was not how it was suppose to go! My dad drove us home that night. Because I had been discharged from the hospital three days early, my body hadn't had time to heal. Every little bump we hit on the 45-minute drive home brought pain and discomfort. My breasts were leaking and my body longed to feed my son. How could this be? I was producing precious milk for my precious baby and he couldn't benefit from it. He was gone. I was in physical and emotional pain and I didn't know what to do with it.

When I walked into our home, my daughters Paige and Marrae (5- and 2-years-old at the time) greeted me with hugs and kisses. It was a joy to see them, and my face almost cracked when I smiled. I cried myself to sleep that night and several nights thereafter.

Ironically on May 24th, my mother's birthday, we were attending Lucas' funeral. I could see the worry and concern in my mom's eyes. I felt sad because this should have been a happy day for her.

The hardest thing for me was/is:

In the beginning I had mixed emotions when I saw pregnant women and mothers with new babies. I felt sincerely happy for them yet envious at the same time.

Picking out his urn was hard. A small room full of urns; different shapes and sizes. It didn't feel real; shopping for an urn for our newborn baby. We should've been at Toy's R Us shopping for a colorful mobile for his crib. We ended up picking out the most beautiful urn we could find, and my husband and I easily agreed. It was a wooden box with a beautiful scene carved in it. It had a beautiful mountain top and sunset.

Another hard thing is missing Lucas every day. Missing the smiles I will never see or the hugs I will never feel. The never-ending unanswered questions: First of all, why? And what would he look like? Would he have thick dark hair like his Dad? What would he be doing? What milestones would he be at? Starting high school? Chasing girls? What would his likes or dislikes be? Would he be playing video games with his brothers or reading and studying with his sisters? What would his voice sound like today? His laugh?

Helpful things that family and friends did that I will forever be grateful for:
A lot of our family members where there with us during Lucas' last hours and we appreciated them being there.

The Neonatal Intensive Care Unit staff at Maine Medical Center in Portland, Maine; they were wonderful in every way. They took photos for us, and supplied cameras so that we could have pictures of Lucas to treasure. They gave us our privacy while we said goodbye and supplied us with a gift box full of his things. We have a lock of his hair, his pacifier, the clothes he was wearing and his baby footprints.

My mom took a week off to stay with me while I was healing, physically and emotionally. She was amazing and helped with everything that needed to be done on a daily basis.

My brother and some of his friends helped move all of the baby furniture and clothes out of our house before we got home. It would have been even more painful to go home and look at an empty crib or to have to look at all the baby clothes that Lucas wouldn't get to wear.

My dad gave Lucas a teddy bear and wrote a nice note to him. It was sweet.

My in-laws were there for us and helped with all the funeral arrangements, which was a huge help. I was in such a daze that I hardly remember it. I don't know what we would've done without them.

A friend of ours, Angela, brought over a nice hot meal one evening. She had prepared lasagna, salad, bread and dessert. It was so thoughtful of her and we loved not having to think about what to make for dinner that evening.

My dear friend, Sylvia, answered questions from work clients who called in to see how my new baby and I were doing. She was the one who explained (so that I didn't have to) that there were complications and that Lucas had passed. I know it wasn't easy for her and I will always appreciate her courage during that time.

Things that have helped me cope and deal with the heartache:

Things that have help ease my pain are: God, praying, writing letters to Lucas, online Infant Loss support groups, reading other peoples stories, helping and supporting others during difficult times with words of comfort, books, books and more books. Also reading books on anything spiritual in nature, grief, life after death, and reading related poems. Talking about Lucas and keeping his memory alive. And keeping a journal helps me to release painful emotions.

What I have learned from this:
I feel as though I have grown and am continually trying to become the best person I can be. I am learning to live in and appreciate the present moment now. I appreciate my children and hearing the sound of their voices. I am thankful for every day I have with them and I tell them so. Because of my experience and losing Lucas, my entire way of thinking changed. With the support of my husband, I made a difficult decision and decided to end my career as a successful office manager working for a global corporation, to being a stay-at-home Mom. It's not always easy. Our entire way of living changed. We now cut coupons and buy almost everything used. It was a frightening choice, but I didn't want to miss out on my children's lives. It goes by so fast and the time can be so short. I was away nine or ten hours a day and missing so much. I have gained that back and feel so fortunate and blessed on a daily basis because of it.

I try to follow my heart and let it guide me. I was drawn to Reiki a few years ago and took all the courses needed to become a Reiki Master/Teacher. I also looked into another healing practice called Integrated Energy Therapy, and took classes required for that as well. I was drawn to church and have been attending regularly. I attended a Women's Retreat with my church and it was a great experience. I took a class the church offered and learned much more about The Word than I'd ever known. I attend a weekly Bible Study group and it's been a powerful experience, and we've even seen some incredible healing within the group. Learning The Word has been a freedom like no other.

I've learned that the light within always outshines the dark. I've learned that I want to continue to grow and expand. I've learned that we are all in this together, and I want to help and support others in as many ways as I can.

How I keep my infant's memory alive:
For years, I included a small photo of Lucas in the bottom corner of our family Christmas card. We also celebrate his birthday each year with cake and ice cream. We sing Happy Birthday to him, and blow out candles. I share his photo on my social network pages with friends and family in his honor. And I have a cabinet with his things in our dining room. His framed birth certificate, stuffed animals, photos, dried flowers, his baby rattles, angel figurines; anything that reminds us of Lucas goes into this cabinet.

Additional words to help others dealing with the loss of their infant:
Take your time healing. Remember that everyone is different. If you feel like crying, cry. Feel your emotions and let them pass when you're ready. Be open to signs from your angel. If you think for a moment that it's a sign, then it is. Don't doubt it. Try to remain positive and keep the faith, knowing that even though we as human beings cannot possibly understand, there is a source far greater than us and

that with love, all will one day fall into place. Helping and supporting others in need will also help with your healing. Let your story inspire and bring comfort to others, because it will.

~Melissa Eshleman ~

"And once the storm is over, you won't remember how you made it through. How you managed to survive. You won't even be sure whether the storm is really over. But one thing is certain. When you come out of the storm, you won't be the same person who walked in."

~ Haruki Murakami

Afterword

You are to be commended for finishing this book. Reading of loss can be difficult. Although nothing will erase your grief, you have just taken an important step towards healing. Taking it one step at a time and day-by-day will lead you on a path of awakening and solace. Grief can sometimes persist and linger. It can return when we least expect it and catch us off guard, therefore, you should keep this book along with other helpful tools handy. Check out the resource section and find additional help if needed. Be patient with yourself and allow yourself time to heal on your own terms and timetable. There is no right or wrong way to grieve. Do what feels right for you. Have faith and be kind to yourself. I wish you peace and comfort.

About Melissa Eshleman

In 2001 Melissa had to say goodbye to her four day old infant son Lucas, who was born with Apert's Syndrome and a heart defect.

Melissa founded Find Your Way Publishing, Inc. with the dream of helping others by publishing works to help people "find their way" in all areas of their lives. Melissa is a member of several infant loss groups and plans on donating several of these books to hospitals and bereaved parents around the country.

Melissa and her husband are blessed to have four wonderful children in their lives that keep them very busy. She enjoys reading, writing, being outdoors, studying the Bible, spending time with her loved ones and learning and applying tools for spiritual growth.

Resources

These are just a few of the resources I've come across over the years. There are so many helpful groups and organizations available to offer support to bereaved parents. Please keep in mind that this is just a small listing. The resources available are unlimited. Where there is help, there is hope.

~ Support & Resources ~

A.M.E.N.D. (Aiding a Mother and Father Experiencing Neonatal Death)
1559 Ville Rosa
Hazelwood, MO 63042
Phone: (314) 291-0892

A Place to Remember
1885 University Avenue, Suite 110
Saint Paul, MN 55104
Phone: (800) 631-0973
Website: www.aplacetoremember.com

American SIDS Institute
528 Raven Way
Naples, FL 34110
Phone: (239) 431-5425
Fax: (239) 431-5536
Website: www.sids.org

Bereaved Parents of the USA
National Office
Post Office Box 95
Park Forest, IL 60466
Phone: (708) 748-7866
Website: www.bereavedparentsusa.org

CJ Foundation for SIDS
HUMC: WFAN Pediatric Center
30 Prospect Avenue
Hackensack, NJ 07601
Tel: (201) 996-5301
Toll Free: (888) 8CJ-SIDS
Fax: (201) 996-5326
Email: info@cjsids.org
Web site: www.cjsids.org

Compassionate Friends
National Office
P.O. Box 3696
Oak Brook IL 60522-3696
Phone: (630) 990-0010
Fax: (630) 990-0246
Website: www.compassionatefriends.org

Faces of Loss, Faces of Hope
Putting a face on miscarriage, stillbirth, and infant loss
PO Box 26131
Minneapolis, MN 55426
Website: www.facesofloss.com

First Candle (previously SIDS Alliance)
1314 Bedford Avenue,
Suite 210
Baltimore, MD 21208
Phone: (800) 221-7437
Email: info@firstcandle.org
Website: www.firstcandle.org

Heartstrings
Pregnancy & Infant Loss Support
PO Box 10825, Greensboro, NC 27404-0825
Phone: (336) 335-9931
Email: info@heartstringssupport.org
Website: www.heartstringssupport.org

Miss Foundation
P.O. Box 5333
Peoria, Arizona 85385
Phone: (623) 979-1000
Fax: (623) 979-1001
Website: www.missfoundation.org

The National Sudden and Unexpected Infant/Child Death and Pregnancy Loss Resource Center
Georgetown University
Box 571272
Washington, DC 20057-1272
Phone: (866) 866-7437
Fax: (202) 784-9777
E-mail: info@sidscenter.org
Website: www.sidscenter.org

Pregnancy and Infant Loss Center
1421 E. Wayzata Blvd.
Wayzata, MN 55391
Phone: (612) 473-9372

Remembering Our Babies
3210 Ewing Drive
Manvel, TX 77578
Website: www.october15th.com

Rowan Tree Foundation
PO Box 393
Parker, CO 80134
Phone: (303) 378-4300
Website: www.rowantreefoundation.org

Share Pregnancy & Infant Loss Support, Inc.
The National Share Office
402 Jackson Street
St. Charles, MO 63301
Phone: (636) 947-6164 or (800) 821-6819
Fax: (636) 947-7486
Website: www.nationalshare.org

~ Additional Internet Resources ~

http://community.babycenter.com/groups/a15155/miscarriage_stillbirth_infant_loss_support

http://www.facebook.com/pages/Pregnancy-Infant-Loss/136487461035

http://health.groups.yahoo.com/group/angelbabies4/

http://health.groups.yahoo.com/group/Infant-Loss/

www.myspace.com/allangelbabies

www.nowisleep.com

~ Resources for Keepsakes ~

A Heart to Hold
PO Box 60954
Sacramento, California 95860
Website: www.ahearttohold.org

A Place To Remember
1885 University Avenue
Suite 110
Saint Paul, MN USA 55104
Phone: (800) 631-0973
FAX (651)-645-4780
Website: www.aplacetoremember.com

Angel Names Association
PO Box 423
Saratoga Springs, New York 12866
Website: www.angelnames.org

Benjamin Ministries
990 Calkins Road
Rochester, NY 14623
Website: www.benjaminministries.org

La Belle Dame
2476 TransCanada Highway
Flat River, PEI
C0A 1B0
Canada
Website: www.labelledame.com

Memorial Jewelry
Held Your Whole Life, Inc.
1012 Lodgepole Court
Powell, WY 82435
Website: www.heldyourwholelife.com

My Forever Child
P.O. Box 541
East Northport, NY 11731
Phone: (888) 325-2828
Website: www.myforeverchild.com

Lil Angels Hankies
Website: www.lilangelshankies.com

Metal Stamped Memories
Website: www.metalstampedmemories.com

Project BEAR Inc.
230 Bethlehem Pike
Colmar, Pennsylvania, 18915
Website: www.projectbear.com

Remembering Our Babies
3210 Ewing Drive
Manvel, TX 77578
Website: www.rememberingourbabies.net

The Comfort Company
1144 East State Street, Suite #A214
Geneva, IL 60134
Phone: (888) 265-2822
Website: www.thecomfortcompany.net

~ Books ~

A Gathering of Angels by Victoria Leland

Angel Marie: The Making of an Angel by Sam Oliver

Always Within: Grieving the Loss of Your Infant by Melissa Eshleman

An Empty Cradle, a Full Heart: Reflections for Mothers and Fathers After Miscarriage, Stillbirth, or Infant Death by Christine O'Keeffe Lafser

Empty Arms: Coping After Miscarriage, Stillbirth and Infant Death by Sherokee Ilse

Empty Cradle, Broken Heart, Revised Edition: Surviving the Death of Your Baby by Deborah L. Davis

Find Peace: Exercises to Help Heal the Pain of a Loss by Brook Noel

Footsteps Through Grief by Darcie Sims

Given In Love But Not Mine To Keep: Finding Strength In The Loss Of A Newborn Child by Jan Wolfe Rosales

Grieving the Child I Never Knew by Kathe Wunnenberg

Healing Your Grieving Heart After Stillbirth: 100 Practical Ideas for Parents and Families by Alan D. Wolfelt

Heaven's Child: Recovering from the loss of an infant by Christine K. Ikenberry

Hope is Like the Sun: Finding Hope and Healing After Miscarriage, Stillbirth, or Infant Death by Lisa Church

In A Heartbeat by Dawn Siegrist Waltman

Journaling Away Mommy's Grief by Robin Lentz Worgan

Life Touches Life: A Mother's Story of Stillbirth and Healing by Lorraine Ash

Living with Grief: A Guide to Your First Year of Grieving by Brook Noel

Losing Malcolm: A Mother's Journey Through Grief by Carol Henderson

Love Never Dies by Sandy Goodman

Mama Mockingbird by Sauni Wood

The Mourner's Book of Courage: 30 Days of Encouragement by Alan Wolfelt

Parting is Not Goodbye by Kelly Osmont

Pregnancy After a Loss: A Guide to Pregnancy After a Miscarriage, Stillbirth, or Infant Death by Carol Cirulli Lanham

Stolen Angels: 25 Stories of Hope After Pregnancy or Infant Loss by Sharee G. Moore

Surviving the Holidays, Birthdays, & Anniversaries by Brook Noel

Tender Fingerprints by Brad Stetson

Transcending Loss: Understanding the Lifelong Impact of Grief & How to Make it Meaningful by Ashley Davis Prend

Waiting with Gabriel: A Story of Cherishing a Baby's Brief Life by Amy Kuebelbeck

Waking Up to This Day by Paula D'Arcy

Waterbugs & Dragonflies: Explaining Death to Young Children by Doris Stickney

What Was Lost: A Christian Journey Through Miscarriage by Elise Erikson Barrett

~ DVD's ~

Enduring Love, Transforming Loss at bereavement-services.org

Footprints on Our Hearts: How to Cope After a Miscarriage, Stillbirth, or Newborn Death at amazon.com or centering.org or griefstore.com

Grieving in the NICU: Mending Broken Hearts When a Baby Dies at grievingforbabies.org

~ Songs ~

All My Tears ~ Selah

Angels Among US - Alabama

Beauty From Pain ~ Superchick

Before The Morning ~ Josh Wilson

Broken ~ Lindsey Haun

Cradle of Wings - In Memory ~ Pam Armstrong and Susan Armstrong Lunn

Fly ~ Celine Dion

Glory Baby ~ Watermark

Godspeed (Sweet Dreams) ~ Dixie Chicks

Goodbye For Now ~ Kathy Troccoli

Heaven Was Needing A Hero ~ Jo Dee Messina

Held ~ Natalie Grant

Hello, Goodbye ~ Michael W. Smith

How Come The World Won't Stop ~ Anastacia

I Believe ~ Diamond Rio

I Can Only Imagine ~ Mercy Me

I Knew I loved You ~ Savage Garden

I Will Carry You (Audrey's Song) ~ Selah

In The Arms Of an Angel ~ Sarah McLaughlin

My Heart Will Go On ~ Celine Dion

My Name ~ George Canyon

One More Day With You ~ Diamond Rio

Precious Child ~ Karen Taylor Good

Smallest, Wingless ~ Craig Cardiff

Still ~ Gerrit Hofsink

To Where You Are ~ Josh Groban

When I Look To The Sky ~ Train

Who You'd Be Today ~ Kenny Chesney

Always Loved

GRIEVING THE LOSS OF A BABY

Disclaimer

The purpose of this book is to provide information about the subject matter covered. The author and publisher shall have neither liability nor responsibility to any person or entity with respect to any loss or damage caused, or alleged to have been caused, directly or indirectly, by the information contained in this book. The stories contained in this book are the contributor's recollections of their experiences. This book is not intended nor is it implied to be a substitute for professional medical advice, and any medical advice, and any medical information contained in this book is not intended to be diagnostic or treatment in any way. The author and publisher are not engaged in rendering medical, psychological or any other professional services. If medical, psychological or other expert assistance is required, please talk to your physician and locate the services of a competent professional. If you do not wish to be bound by the above, you may return this book along with a copy of the receipt to the publisher for a full refund.

Always Loved

GRIEVING THE LOSS OF A BABY

Quick Order Form

Telephone orders: 207-739-9640

Internet orders: www.findyourwaypublishing.com

Postal orders: Find Your Way Publishing, Inc.
PO Box 667
Norway, ME 04268
USA

Please include:

Name of book:

Quantity:

Your Name:

Address:

City:

State:

Zip:

Telephone:

Email address:

Always Loved

GRIEVING THE LOSS OF A BABY

Quick Order Form

Telephone orders: 207-739-9640

Internet orders: www.findyourwaypublishing.com

Postal orders: Find Your Way Publishing, Inc.
PO Box 667
Norway, ME 04268
USA

Please include:

Name of book:

Quantity:

Your Name:

Address:

City:

State:

Zip:

Telephone:

Email address:

www.ingramcontent.com/pod-product-compliance
Lightning Source LLC
Chambersburg PA
CBHW071707090426
42738CB00009B/1697